WHAT OTHERS ARE SAYING ABOUT "ABOVE THE CHATTER OUR WORDS MATTER."

...On countless mornings prior to scrubbing for my first heart operation on a tiny baby, while standing at the scrub sink, I have read the words penned by Bruce and been motivated, inspired, focused, and calmed. WORDS are POWER.... and this book contains powerful words that will have the same kind of influence on countless others.

Jeffrey P. Jacobs, MD, Professor of Surgery,
Johns Hopkins University

... Bruce's messages and his commitment to this meaningful project have been motivating to me personally, and I am certain that many others will be taken to higher levels of happiness and achievement by his inspirational messages.

James Paschal, Head Golf Professional,
General Manager, Gaylord Springs Golf Links

...*Above the Chatter, Our Words Matter,* allows us to reach within, find answers and achieve higher state of awareness and greatness. Bruce's "can do"attitude and passion to make a difference by supporting others through difficult times makes this book inspirational and uplifting for anyone who reads it.

Andrea Rosenthal, Counselor & Business Coach,
Life and Career Soulutions

ABOVE THE CHATTER, OUR WORDS MATTER

ABOVE THE CHATTER, OUR WORDS MATTER

POWERFUL WORDS THAT CHANGED MY LIFE FOREVER

BRUCE PULVER

Above the Chatter, Our Words Matter

Published by Clovercroft Publishing, Franklin, Tennessee

Cover Design by Madoka Oshima

Interior Design by Adept Content Solutions

Edited by Tammy Kling

Printed in the United States of America

978-1-942557-23-4

DEDICATION

Words are powerful! The messages in this book and the daily inspiration I received from writing and working to live by them have ABSOLUTELY changed my life.

With the support from my wife, Brigette, and daughters, Payton and Emily, I wrote this book to help others focus and commit to using positive words and thoughts when talking to ourselves and with others. I am convinced that positive words lead to the most favorable outcomes and experiences. My family is the source of my drive and motivation. Every day I see their zest for life, relentless love, and powerful possibility thinking.

My parents, Arthur and Dorothy Pulver, passed too soon yet taught me so much. I dedicate these messages to them for the positive foundation they gave me to handle life's challenges. My bright memory of them fuels my strength each day, in every life situation, and in all decisions I make. God blessed me with their presence and with the gift of the following messages in a time of my greatest need.

ACKNOWLEDGEMENTS

At the risk of missing many, I must acknowledge a few who played key roles in this project and in my life.

Madoka Oshima, you listened to my passion about these words being a gift and you captured my vision with your art. For both your creative mind and patient spirit, I thank you.

Donna S. Pugliese erased my worries about format and content layout. Thank you for your attention to detail.

Mike Hobbs, thank you for advice about taking proper care of these messages.

Andrea Rosenthal of "Career Soulutions," you spoke of success for me at a time when I failed to see it. You inspired me to muster the courage to always believe in myself.

Melissa Gordon, of Echelon Communicate, you gave me specific guidance during a key transition period for me. Your insight is always spot-on and perfectly timed.

Dominick DeRosa and Amy Sebero, you offered me a place to land and helped me seize the opportunity to succeed professionally again. You are masters at creating the setting and the support needed for your team to achieve at high levels. You are incredible leaders.

Tammy Kling, Tiarra Thompkins, and Larry Carpenter, you each embraced this project unconditionally from our first meeting. Thank you for joining my team and guiding me. You have enabled me to attain my goal of getting my message of the power of words available to help others. Your encouragement and enthusiasm was essential and invaluable for me to push and complete my work.

To my dear friend, Russell Kohl, you have taught me about the importance of seeking clarity. I cherish every moment and every conversation with you.

Thank you, James Paschal. Our thirty-plus-year friendship started with you teaching me so much more than golf on the practice tee. I have learned that life will teach us lesssons if we just "pay attention." Thank you for the joyful walks down many fairways.

Your words matter

so use them well.

CONTENTS

The two most important days
in your life are the day
you are born and the day
you find out why.

—Mark Twain

INTRODUCTION

The day I was born could have been the worst day of my life. But instead it was the best.

My mother suffered a "dissecting aneurysm of the aorta" during labor with me. I literally broke her heart. From what the history of this medical trauma taught me, seventy-three cases were on record from 1798 and my mother's case in 1961. Of these cases, nineteen patients died within one hour, another twenty-nine passed away between one and forty-eight hours, and the remaining twenty-five survived longer and were placed in a category of subacute. Eleven died within ten days, eight more within ten weeks, four were titled chronic or healed, and as of the report referenced (*New England Journal of Medicine*, January 24, 1962), only two patients were living. My mother was one of them. My mother's heart was revived, healed, and transformed.

She believed every day thereafter was a blessing, a gift to be celebrated by being thankful for the miracle she was given. My father, who was the silent patient in this ordeal, called on his faith and had the support of family and friends to help his strength grow while being tested each moment.

I am blessed with parents who believed in the blessings of life and embraced them. Never dwelling on the negative, I lived in a home that embraced the joy of living and the grace they believe they received during that period.

The Wake-Up Call

What kind of grace have you received in your life? Grace is like a wake-up call.

One day, I emerged from a deep sleep, and a single word hit me—STRONG. My mind was focused on S-T-R-O-N-G. The puzzle had to be solved. As I became fixed on defining STRONG using just these six letters, the result was: "Stand /Tall / Remain / Optimistic / Now / Go (for it)." Relentlessly repeating the word in my head, I reached for pen and paper to capture this message. The power of concentration was riveting. What just happened? Where did this come from? I have always been drawn to my father's intrigue for words and strived to see life's positives just like my mother. Never had I seen these interests as anything special.

In an instant two parts of my personality were fused. From that day forward, **every morning for four hundred straight days,** a new word and message came to me. I used each new daily message to drive my attitude and focus. Each word helped retool the way I dealt with daily challenges, pressures, and difficult circumstances. The words on the pages that follow are organized by themed chapters to offer a helpful message for specific situations. **The 400-day ritual of receiving these words taught me that the power of a single word can dramatically change thoughts, attitudes, intentions, behavior, and ultimately, LIFE.**

Life at that Moment

When facing the reality of a job loss and being the main income source for our family, that S-T-R-O-N-G moment in time kicked in the survival instinct. I needed strength for my family and myself. I had to develop a mind-set of action that would lift me to a positive place. S-T-R-O-N-G was exactly what I needed to hear and to be. This freakish morning experience turned into a daily routine.

Though it was scary at first, I quickly realized this was a gift and blessing for starting each day. Finding a new word to set my direction and to share with my family became my way of being STRONG and focused in spite of what was going on around me. With each new word and new day, I strived to live the positive message it contained. Each new message provided the clarity and strength to believe in myself and to move forward. This experience was a gift that the cover design of a gift box demonstrates. And I wanted to share this gift, one which I embraced, nurtured—and most importantly, believed—with others.

In life, you'll have gifts and wake-up calls. The wake-up calls are pivotal moments that will show you things you've never known before. Capture them and use them for the world.

You'll also have close calls, like my mother, near misses that make you appreciate the value of each day. Your life matters. Make the most of each moment and let the words within this book speak to your heart.

When the words for this book came to me, the messages appeared clearly and completely. My notepad filled easily—almost as if the messages were passing directly through me onto the paper. What resulted was the drive to face each day and to become stronger. These words provided the energy to drive the action I needed.

In retrospect, this 400-day experience made a rough period smoother, a dark period brighter, and provided focus on being BETTER, not BITTER. It helped see POSSIBILITIES and lifted my spirit each day. I understand now this gift's impact on my life. Through receiving it, I gained the strength to stay positive and expect a great outcome.

While facing my challenges, this gift has also taught our family that good can come from difficult situations if a positive and expectant outlook is used to believe in ourselves. The words we choose to speak to ourselves and to others ABOSLUTELY matter.

Through the encouragement of my family and friends, a book that shares these messages became a natural extension of receiving my gift. The title *Above the Chatter, Our Words Matter* just seemed right. My goal? I will have succeeded if a single message:

- lends an encouraging hand,
- helps one person overcome a challenge or a personal struggle,
- helps others attain the courage to start a new journey in life, or
- leads to greater personal achievement.

It is intended to provide a message of possibility and inspiration to others just as I experienced in "real time."

We all have our own stories of life's disappointments and set-backs. Many of us are dealing with them right now. My wish is for these messages to help others overcome their fears, issues, challenges, and/or insecurities and soar to new heights. May each reader find a word and message that leads to his/her own greatness.

There are sixteen chapters organized about believing in one-self, getting started, recharging, staying strong, managing un-controllable circumstances, celebrating one's uniqueness, and managing one's attitudes and emotions. Each day of the week and each month of the year are represented as well.

Please find your own way to use these this book. I sincerely hope it will impact every reader in a way that provides inspiration and a determination to move forward with a positive, can-do intention. Above all the crazy chatter in our lives, the words we choose to speak to ourselves and out loud really do matter.

Intensely focus on learning
the rules of the game.
You are then able to decide
how you will play it.
Time spent listening to others
on how to play the game is
fruitless when it comes to
deciding your strategy.
Your uniqueness is
your strength.

POSITIVE AFFIRMATION: GETS THE DOUBT OUT

Attitude and mindset dictate personal outlook in all situations. Think you can, you can. Think you can't, you can't. If you go into a situation with a negative outlook, don't expect a positive outcome. I first learned this in sporting and music events as a child. Whenever I thought I *could* do something, I always had a better outcome. Attitude is quite different from nervousness. Being nervous shows a desire to do well in uncertain circumstances. Attitude is an overriding belief and state of mind relating to one's disposition. One might be nervous about an upcoming sporting match or vocal performance, but the player/artist with the positive attitude toward the challenge is best positioned to overcome nervousness and to do well.

YES, I CAN
Ever since our daughters were toddlers, we encouraged them to say, "YES, I CAN," when they faced something new such as climbing the ladder, riding a bike, jumping off a diving board, trying out for a team, or working on a theater part. These words give a positive mental expectation and a sense of calm confidence.

Y ou
E xpect
S uccess

I n

C hallenging
A ctivities
N OW!

Say these words sometime today!

SELF TALK

SELF TALK is powerful. Words we speak to ourselves dictate our attitude, self-confidence, self-perception, and outcomes. Choose carefully.

S elect possibility words
E xclude never and can't
L et go of NO
F oster self-encouragement

T ell yourself, "YES, I will"
A llow yourself to deserve success
L oosen performance-pressure words
K eep the conversation uplifting

DECLARE

Life often requires significant changes along the way (career, relationship, health, etc.). One step that helps drive the change needed and desired it is to **DECLARE** to ourselves.

D ecide what change we want
E ducate ourselves on what it takes
C ommit to achieve the outcome
L et us believe in ourselves
A sk God for guidance and strength
R ecommit if we prefer to quit
E nvision ourselves living the change

JOURNEY

Each day requires another step in life's **JOURNEY**. Strive to make the most of each day.

J ump in, it's waiting for me
O pening myself to possibilities
U sing my gifts to give and grow
R emembering yesterday is gone
N o promise I will get tomorrow
E xpecting a great day today
"Y es, I can" is the mantra

What will make your day's JOURNEY a great one?

JOYRNEY
Here's a variation on journey.

J ump for Joy for no reason
O ptimism is the wingman
Y ou have God given gifts—use them
R each out to others
N o regrets along the way
E njoy each step
Y ou now have a JOURNEY

It's all about the *U*'s and *Y*'s of it. Find your JOY in the JOYRNEY.

TODAY: A Double Dose
One way to face TODAY or What to do about TODAY?

T ake	T ackle
O ptimistic	O pportunities
D irection	D eliberatley
A chieve	A ffirming
Y our dreams	Y our success

THRIVE
In all we do, we deserve to **THRIVE**. But it takes work and commitment.

T ake on the challenge with passion
H ave the belief you can do it
R eally work hard toward the goal
I nspiration comes from progress
V isualize the achievement
E xperience the joy of accomplishment

SHARPER
Not every day can be SHARP. Sometimes we have days that make us appreciate the good ones. Tomorrow, I will be **SHARPER**.

S tart with thanks for my blessings
H andle with joy and positive outlook
A ttune to possibilities
R efocused on what's important
P repared to face challenges
E ager to solve problems
R ely on faith—God is with me

REFLECTION
When looking in the mirror in the morning, we can make our own RE-
FLECTION.

R eady for the day
E xpect challenges along the way
F ace whatever comes today
L ook for something positive
E ngage and take action
C atch a little sunshine today
T ake action toward our goals
I nsist on staying focused
O pen with a smile
N ever give up

FOR YOU
Make time today FOR YOU.

F ind some time and a place
O kay, now escape for a moment
R eflect on something you cherish

Y ou deserve a short getaway
O nly focused on you
U se these moments to strengthen

START AND KEEP MOVING:
TAKE THE FIRST STEP

It has been said that 50 percent of accomplishing a goal is to just SHOW UP. Getting started on a goal can ignite the momentum to achieve the desired outcome or change. This is true for learning a new skill, shedding those unwanted pounds, or getting back to the love of painting. The first step might be laying out your workout clothes at the foot of the bed at night, so they are there for you in the morning. Tell yourself step one is to GET STARTED.

MOTIVATION
MOTIVATION means taking the first step and then staying with it.

M ove first, don't question
O pen the mind to possibilities
T ake the first step of initiative
I nvest in yourself
V isualize the desired outcome
A sk if not me, then who?
T ake action
I nternalize the inspiration to improve
O ptimism from the start
N ever doubt possibilities

MOTIVATED
Here's how to get and stay **MOTIVATED**. When seeking something new that improves your life try this:

M ake progress your daily goal
O rient yourself for the long haul
T ake little steps and celebrate them
I nternally cheer you each day
V isualize the end state
A cknowledge you are improving
T alk to a buddy who is encouraging
E liminate defeatist thinking
D o it until you get it then raise the goal

WAITING
What are we **WAITING** for?

W hy are we hesitating?
A re we afraid of failure?
I f we don't try we have already failed
T ake a chance, it beats standing still
I f we are not happy, it's up to us
N othing changes if we don't
G et more, do more

Double Take — ACTION and TAKE ACTION
To clearly see what we want is critical. To take the **ACTION** to attain it is essential.

ACTION
A re we willing to do the work?
C an we sustain the change required?
T ake "out with the old, in with the new" focus
I s the desired result greather than the pain of change?
O nly we can make it happen
N ow there is clarity with reality

TAKE ACTION
Nothing we want happens until we **TAKE ACTION**.

T alk less, do more
A ct on what we want
K eep moving toward the goal
E ye the target

A ccept the challenge
C ount on yourself and work for it
T ake setbacks in stride
I ntensify the calm in the moment
O wn the outcome
N ow get going

START
When we feel trapped wanting to do something new, but don't know where to begin, just **START**.

S et your sites on your target
T ake the first of many steps
A djust as needed but keep moving
R each farther each day
T akes a little belief in yourself

NOW
More often than not regret comes from nonaction rather than from actions taken. So, the question to ask ourselves is: If not **NOW**, when?

N o more waiting, go for it
O wning my intentions
W orking hard on what matters

DO
We feel better when we say less and **DO** more. Potential new meaning for a to-**DO** list.

D ive in with high energy
O wn actions that only improve the situation

JUMP
Often the first step needed for the improvement desired is to **JUMP** in and begin.

J ust say you can and you will
U se your mind, heart, and soul
M ake the commitment to action
P rogress each day is the measure

GAIN
To **GAIN** what we want in life, we must:

G et committed to what is required
A ct daily in the direction we want
I nsist on doing everything it takes
N ever give up

PUSHING
Ever been excited about a new opportunity but have to close out a current role first? It can be difficult to stay motivated in the current role or task. A coworker asked me about this recently. The reply? "Just keep **PUSHING**."

P resent is the priority
U nderstand it's temporary
S ee it through—you'll feel better
H ave fun with your transition
I nsist on finishing
N ew opportunity is around the corner
G ive it all you got

MOVING
We are always MOVING, but it's important to be moving with purpose.

M otion with motivation
O riented toward specific goals
V igorously passioned
I ntentional with actions
N ot to be denied
G iving unstoppable effort

Keep MOVING.

Twice the TRACTION
Sometimes we can get in a rut. The wheels spin with no TRACTION. Is it possible to create our own TRACTION? Yes, I say!

T ake a hold of the journey
R ealize that the direction we are going may be the problem
A lways stay positive
C reate little steps to get movement
T ry something new, the old stuff isn't working
I f it's gonna be, it's up to me
O bserve, opportunities abound
N ow get back in gear, try again

TRACTION
Athletes wear cleated shoes to dig in and get TRACTION. On getting TRACTION in life's journey:

T otal focus on the task at hand
R eaching far with each stride
A ttitude of determination
C ommitment to completion
T akes sacrificing the "easy way out"
I nternal drive and inspiration is key
O ptimism when things look down
N ow dig in and go for it

STEP
To make progress to our goals, we must take the first STEP.

S tart with the END in mind
T ake responsibility and accountability
E mpower yourself with confidence
P repare to work harder than ever

LAUNCH
How to **LAUNCH** ourselves forward:

L et nothing hold you back
A ccept current status as only temporary
U nleash your energy to move ahead
N ever let anyone or anything convince you that you cannot
C laim your goals
H ave determination to get there

TRIGGERS
Mental **TRIGGERS** can help us perform and stay focused. A short self- message that helps zoom in on an important effort. An example of TRIGGER is "I GOT THIS."

T ake a step away from it all
R eset the intention
I t can be done—one step at atime
G et on with just the task at hand
G ive it full attention
E ngage in the moment
R elaxation enables performance
S et ourselves on GO

SUSTAIN
We all can make a change to improve ourselves. How do we **SUSTAIN** the change once we achieve it, i.e. weight loss, exercise programs, healthy eating, and relationship growth?

S ay, "I will keep this going."
U se positive self-talk to stay on track
S ay daily sustaining affirmations
T ake pride in the result you've attained
A ccept your new self as who you are
I like this result more than I dislike the work to keep it
N ow set a new goal!

URGENCY
Having a sense of sense of **URGENCY** can actually be calming.

U se time to plan and prioritize
R efuse to panic
G et to what matters quickly
E nergize on the important items
N ullify meaningless distractions
C almly commit to focus
Y ou can now get to what matters

STRIVE
Some of the most consistent high performers stay in a continuous loop
of striving to improve. They seem to thrive in the **STRIVE**.

S imply focuses on improvement
T akes out the performance anxiety
R eaches farther each day
I nsists on being in the present
V alidates from effort, not outcome
E xpects progress, not perfection

REPEAT*
Achieving success the second time at the same activity is very different
from the first. There is much more pressure to make it happen again.
Consider how hard it is to repeat great grades, a second great performance of the same piece of music, earning a championship in the same
event two years in a row. Here is one way to think about it:

R emember the legacy
E xpect adversity
P repare tirelessly
E levate confidently
A ttack relentlessly
T ackle the challenge proudly

*Written for the Pace Academy Lady Knights Varsity Soccer Team after
winning the Georgia State High School Division I-A State Championship on May 17, 2014.*

KEEP IT SIMPLE: BE CLEAR, BE CONCISE, AND SEEK PERSPECTIVE

Often we think we must have all the answers and have every conceivable possibility covered or we will be unsuccessful. We can also get ourselves so deep in the details that we forget about the initial idea sparking our passion at first. Seeking simplicity and clarity of purpose helps keep perspective. Sure, at times the detail and complexity will require our energy and focus as we navigate the tricky and intricate aspects of an endeavor. It is equally important to come up for air regularly and remind ourselves to keep things in perspective? Think "UP PARASCOPE!"

CLARITY
A key to happiness, meaning, and purpose in life is **CLARITY**. If missing a clear direction, focus, understanding, or expectation, the path feels obstructed and distracted, seek **CLARITY**.

C learly
L ook
A t
R eality
I nsistent (on)
T ruth (for)
Y ourself

ADAPT
The ability to **ADAPT** to change might be more valuable than the desire to prevent it.

A ccepting that change is a reality
D eclaring change is now constant
A cknowledge survival depends on it
P lanning for the uncertain of it
T raining to **ADAPT** to it

KEYS
KEYS to a great day:

K eep focused on the positive
E xpect hard work and do it
"Y es, I can" attitude
S ee the outcome desired

"Key in" to these KEYS.

REALITY
Part of **REALITY** is being REAL. Do so and it's totally is up to you. So:

R each into your heart and soul
E xpress yourself totally
A chieve what you perceive
L ove yourself and love others
I t's
T otally up to
Y ou

FOCUS
When we have the need to really **FOCUS**, we can often feel a tightening tension in the mind and body, which can restrict us. A friend advised that **FOCUS** and concentration is actually about relaxing and "paying attention" to the moment.

F irst decide what is important
O pen yourself completely to this
C alm awareness becomes the center
U nplug the performance pressure
S eek relaxed awareness, now GO!

Thank you, James Paschal, my dear friend, golf instructor, and life teacher.

BELONG
When we reach a place where we **BELONG**.

B eing there is a great feeling
E veryone accepts you "as is"
L ife moves in a meaningful way
O ne unified sense of purpose
N othing external throws you off
G ood gets great

Seek places to **BELONG** and help others find their belonging place.

FLOURISH
We all have struggled, we deserve to **FLOURISH**. We flourish when we:

F ind inspiring opportunities
L ook for ways to contribute
O pen ourselves to learning
U se ears more than mouth
R espect hard work
I nsist on our best efforts
S ettle for less, NEVER
H ave realism and optimism

Let's all **FLOURISH**!

WHY
Ask **WHY** more often and see where the conversation and thought process goes.

W hy should I take things at face value?
H aving an inquisitive sense frees the mind
Y is a letter AND a question

TRANSITION
There are times in life that require us to **TRANSITION**, work, relationships, etc. Deal with it by seeing it, embracing it, and working with it.

T ime for a change
R ealize the need to adapt
A nticipation allows for preparation
N ow is the opportunity to grow
S eek help from those we respect
T ake control of what we can
I nspire into action
O pen to opportunities
N avigate through the challenges

Thank you, Melissa Gordon and Andrea Rosenthal, for helping me with a major **TRANSITION**.

INSPIRED

Life is so much more fulfilling when we are **INSPIRED**. Being **IN-SPIRED** means:

I ntense about something we find important
N ow is the time to get on it
S ense of urgency like never before
P ositive we will make it happen
I nsisting on making a change for the good
R efusing to go back to an uninspired state
E ngaged with our whole selves
D etermined to exceed expectations

Let's get and fight to stay **INSPIRED**!

CAN I? or **I CAN!**

CAN I or I CAN is simply about order, perspective, and punctuation.

C autious
A nxious
N ervous

I nsecure

or

I nspired

C onfident
A ffirmed
N ever a doubt

MOMENT

We make the best progress when we get in and stay in the **MOMENT**, free from yesterday and letting tomorrow come in time.

M ake it about NOW
O nly tackle the present
M ake the task at hand THE task
E mpower relaxed focus
N otice nothing else
T otal immersion

STEADY
Life can become overwhelming with its rapid change and fast-paced demands. Work to stay **STEADY** in an increasingly hectic world, telling yourself:

S tay true to your heart
T alk positively to yourself
E xpress yourself confidently
A ppreciate your pace
D eal with things calmly
Y ou'll be just fine

PEACEFUL
May everyone have a **PEACEFUL** day.

P ause with intent
E xhale, inhale deeply and repeat
A cknowledge the release
C almness from the inside
E mbrace this space
F ocus on clarity
U nleash the stress
L ive in the moment

BEAUTY
Find **BEAUTY** in today.

B alance
E nergy
A cceptance
U nderstanding
T rusting
Y outhful heart

PERSPECTIVE
Here's a lesson from my father about keeping things in **PERSPECTIVE**.

P lace the situation in the big picture
E valuate the magnitude through the lens
R estrain the emotion of the moment
S ettle the mind to seek clarity
P eacefully determine the relevance
E valuate the alternatives of action
C hoose with a clear mind
T ake your time, trust yourself, and be decisive
I n the grand scheme, how does this measure in importance?
V alidation reveals itself in time
E xamine your perspective and learn from it

PERFECT

Being **PERFECT**. What does that mean? Can we be **PERFECT**? Is that a realistic goal? Major League baseball players with a lifetime successful batting average of .300 get into the Hall of Fame. Thomas Edison failed more often than not before he succeeded with the light bulb. So how about a new focus on being **PERFECT**?

P repare ourselves
E xpect the best outcome
R ehearse (physically and mentally)
F ocus in the moment
E xhale (calms and clears the mind)
C onfidence (you are prepared)
T rust in yourself

Make perfect about preparation, not the outcome.

LISTEN

A wise man once said, "Becoming a better listener makes you a better communicator. One key is to focus and remember, it's about them, not about me." He said, "When someone speaks about something important to them, LISTEN and then ask a question."

L ock
I nto
S omeone (else's)
T otally
E xciting
N ews

VISION

We must develop a clear **VISION** of what we will accomplish. Try this approach: keep it simple and stay focused. (This is a note to self.)

V isualization
I nsight
S implification
I ncreases
O pportunities
N ow

DIRECTION
Seek clear DIRECTION in important endeavors.

D eliberate
I ntensity
R eal
E nergy
C oncentration
T o
I mprove
O perations
N ow

LESS = MORE
In writing, in music, and in design, a common mantra is LESS = MORE.
What about applying this to relationships?

L istening
E ncouraging
S incerely
S upporting

M akes
O ur
R elationships
E nriching

BELIEVE
To achieve our goals, it is vital to BELIEVE we can. A simple strategy to
help is to visualize success in the mind first. See ourselves achieving the
goal. Do this early and often. Seeing success before achieving it helps to
BELIEVE.

B egin
E verything
L ooking
I nside
E xpecting
V isualizing
E xcellence

DAILY
A clear plan for DAILY action.

D ecide to live each day expecting positive outcomes
A ct each day and do your best regardless of the situation
I nsist on praying every day for strength and guidance
L et's be thankful each day regardless
Y ield equals effort

STRIDE
Take things in STRIDE.

S tay true to your dreams
T ackle challenges with unyielding effort
R id yourself of doubt
I nject your will
D ecide, dedicate and do
E xpect struggles—work for success

Take today in STRIDE.

FULFILLED
Live your life FULFILLED.

F ind
U plifting
L ively
F ascinating
I nvolved
L ife-changing
L asting
E xperiences
D aily

DIET
The DIET of Life is about what we eat, read, see, hear, say, and believe. Anything we internalize in our body and mind has an impact. To have a healthy DIET of Life, we must:

D iligently decide what we let in
I ngest only what is healthy
E liminate negative foods, messages, thoughts, and outlooks
T ake control of our Diet of Life

EQUILIBRIUM
To fight the "seesaw" of life's challenges, seek an **EQUILIBRIUM**.

E asy does it
Q uiet time to find your center
U ninhibitedly doing your passion
I nstinctively seek your purpose
L isten to and follow your heart
I nsist on honoring your beliefs
B alance you are happy with
R ejoice in what is joyful
I nvest to revitalize yourself
U nless it inspires you, don't do it
M ean what you do and do what you love

TERRIFIED
Feeling TERRIFIED? Take control and say:

T oo committed to fail
E xactly where I want to be
R eady to face anything
R esponsible for myself
F ace any challenge with confidence
I mpossible to defeat
E xpect to face terrifying situations
D etermined beyond belief

SKEPTICS
SKEPTICS waste their energy trying to hold doers back. They:

S it and judge others
K eep from ever taking a chance
E njoy seeing others fall short
P ass on any risk for fear of failure
T alk a big game but never play
I nsult those that put in the effort
C riticize everything and everyone
S hould either put up or shut up

Here is to the DOERS!

NEVER
Remember that folks who believe in **NEVER** are:

N ot willing to fight through obstacles
E asily willing to give up
V astly underdetermined
E mpowering self-defeat
R eally missing out on opportunities

Don't believe in **NEVER!**

WORTHY
Always believe we are **WORTHY.**

W ere made by God in his image
O n this earth for good reason
R emarkable as we are
T ruly ONE OF A KIND!
H ere to make a real difference
Y es, we must believe and go for our dreams

WORRY
Getting rid of **WORRY**—why?

W orthless use of energy
O nly holds us back
R eaches new levels of despair
R emoves us from the present
Y ields nothing good

Our outcomes are determined
by how we control ourselves
in uncontrollable situations.
Use your AWESOME energy
to control what you can and
forget the rest.

Cop Out?

No, I say control your actions
and watch the circumstances
improve.

4 |

GET REAL: ASPIRE, PERSPIRE, AND ACQUIRE

If all things are equal in terms of preparation and hard work, often the outcome is determined by *who wants it more*. We see this at ALL levels of competition. Winners go the extra mile by pushing when there seems to be no push left and giving the situation the additional effort to figure out a better way to solve a problem. It all starts with the genuine desire to want a better outcome. Next comes the willingness to do whatever it takes to get there.

HOW BADLY WE WANT IT + HOW HARD WE ARE WILLING TO WORK FOR IT = THE RESULT WE GET!

ZEST
Have a ZEST for life. Tackle it with:

Z ebra-stripe uniqueness, embraced
E xcitement of a child, fostered
S trong values, defended
T enacious about chasing dreams

Let's get zesty about life today.

SOAR
To accomplish more, we must dare to **SOAR**.

S ee yourself living our dreams and dedicating ourselves to achieving them
O pen our mind to "no limits"
A spire and NEVER sell ourselves short of our goals
R each the wings of imagination farther than imaginable

SAIL
Ask ourselves, if we could set **SAIL** for anything we wish, where would we go?

S et our sites on what we want
A im our energy at our sites
I magine ourselves living our dreams
L et's believe and go for it

IMPROVE
If we **IMPROVE** one little thing about life each day, what a difference we can make for ourselves and others.

I nsist on getting better
M ake today matter
P ush our limits each day
R efuse to accept status quo
O bstacles are often self-imposed
V alue the contributions we make
E xpect more and do more

ASPIRATION
If we live with **ASPIRATION**, we will be an inspiration.

A pproaching all with positive
S howing our passion
P ushing ourselves to grow
I nquiring, inquiring, and inquiring
R eaching for new goals
A iming for the bullseye
T elling ourselves we CAN
I nsisting on making a difference
O pening doors for ourself and others
N avigating uncertainty with a smile

PERSPIRE
To reach what we desire, we must be willing to **PERSPIRE**.

P repare body and mind for the challenge
E xercise both
R epeat with intent
S ettle only for your best
P ut in more than the work required
I nspire yourself any way you have to
R emember most won't do the work
E xpect it to be hard and enjoy the achievement

LUCK
Have you ever noticed that good LUCK seems to follow those that are well prepared? Coincidence?

L ook optimistically for desired results
U se your energy and resources to prepare everyday
C hallenge yourself to always go the extra mile
K eep working hard with positive attitude and watch how lucky you
   become

WATCH ME
When others say you can't, say to yourself, "WATCH ME!"

Then:

W ork harder
A lways stay positive
T ell yourselves, "I will."
C an do and will do
H ide your drive with humility

M ake obstacles the motivations
E xpect the outcome you want

GET DOING
To GET something different, we must DO something different. Let's GET DOING!

G et a hold of our goals
E xpect work will be required
T ake responsibility for our actions

D edicate ourselves to our objectives
O rganize our efforts
I nspire ourselves
N ever give up
G o the extra mile that others won't go

HARD WORK
My dad told me the key to success is **HARD WORK**.

H ave the will to do what it takes
A dvocate for myself
R ally when the chips are down
D o what others won't

W hen people doubt me, rise up
O rder myself to do more
R ely on ME to make a difference
K now that HARD WORK is it

TENACIOUS
Be **TENACIOUS** about our purpose.

T ake personal ownership
E nergize our spirit
N urture our passion
A ssert ourself
C hallenge our limits
I nquire relentlessly
O wn personal responsibility
U se our unique gifts
S ettle only for our best

GOALS
A great deal is written about the importance of setting **GOALS**. I am a
believer in the power of goal setting.

G ets life aligned for achievement
O rganize with specific written intentions and timeframes
A ctionable and motivating
L eads to a more focused, directed purpose
S ets the mind, body, and spirit in motion together

GROWING
Life is about **GROWING**.

G et
R olling
O n
W hat
I nspires
N ew
G oals

TARGET
To hit your mark, focus on a very specific **TARGET** and

T ake dead aim
A ssess the surroundings
R eaffirm your commitment
G ive it your all
E xhale for calmness
T rust in yourself

DREAMS 1
Achieve our **DREAMS**.

D ecide what you really want in life
R esolve to do the work required
E xpect challenges
A ct with persistent purpose
M ake sacrifices necessary
S ee yourself living your **DREAMS**

DREAMS 2
How **DREAMS** become reality:

D edication to goals
R efuse to let go of them
E mpowered by commitment
A cknowledge it's up to ME
M ake them happen
S hare success by teaching others

DREAMS 3
Commit to **DREAMS**. Let's all recommit to our **DREAMS**. After all, our **DREAMS** are what make us unique from others!

D aily
R eenforcing
E xtraordinary
A ccomplishments
M ade
S ure, to come true

EFFORT
Always give the best **EFFORT**.

E nergy
F ortitude
F aith
O ptimism
R esilience
T enacity

FORWARD
Standing still is actually backing up. Keep moving **FORWARD** to our goals.

F ocus
O n
R eally
W hat
A dvances the
R ight
D eliverables

THRIVE
We are all here to **THRIVE**.

T ake on the day
H ead held high
R each for the stars
I nvest in ourselves
V alue the journey
E njoy the fruits of the labor

FULLEST
Live life to the **FULLEST**.

F ind and follow our passion
U nwavering self respect
L ove of self and others
L ook for the good in everything
E xperience life with positive outlook
S et goals and stay focused on them
T ake risks and believe in ourselves

INTENTIONS
A dear friend once asked me, "What are your life's **INTENTIONS**?"
I took a few days and defined them based on following criteria:

I ntrinsically focused
N ew boundaries of possibility
T est my "normal"
E mpower my passions
N ourish my soul
T each me new life skills
I mprove the lives I touch
O ffer support to others
N urture a universal need
S eek to better the world as I better myself

PUSH
PUSH ourselves to accomplish more.

P ut
U p
S ome
H ard work

IMAGINE
IMAGINE life as we want it, then commit ourselves to making it happen.

I nsist on our own commitment
M aintain dedication to our goals
A pply our heart, mind, and soul
G et help and guidance from experts
I ncremental movement is all we will get on some days—celebrate it
N ever give up if we really want the life we IMAGINE
E xpect the results to equal the work we put in

FOCUS 1
Today requires FOCUS.

F inding
O ne's
C enter
U nwavering
S itck-to-it-ness

FOCUS 2
With so many distractions, it is often quite challenging to keep a FO-CUS. Try this:

F ind out what's important
O rganize our efforts
C oncentrate our energy
U tilize our resources wisely
S tay committed to the objective

ACTION
To make things happen, we must take **ACTION**.

A ll we need to do is start
C hoose our direction and go
T ackle the goal relentlessly
I nsist on a commitment to ourself
O ne intentional step at a time
N ow adjust and keep going

FORTITUDE
Boil down **FORTITUDE** to its elements.

F ind our source of strength
O utwork our fears
R each into the scary place
T ell ourselves we CAN
I mplode the status quo
T ell ourselves we WILL
U se our inspirations
D ecide we will not stop
E xhale, believe, and keep going

FINISH 1*
Much is written about getting started. Once we find the courage to start, put in the hard work it takes to **FINISH**.

F ind the will to dig deep
I nsist on doing whatever it takes
N ever ever give up
I ncrease the intensity to new levels
S tretch efforts beyond expectation
H oist the trophy in the end

FINISH 2
F ind courage to reach the goal
I ncrease the effort to get there
N ow push harder and harder
I ntensify the desire
S cream to ourselves, "I want this"
H ave belief we WILL succeed

Written for the Pace Academy 2014 Girls State Soccer Champions.

5

TWO NEGATIVES ≠
A POSITIVE:
THE ART OF ATTITUDE

In elementary school, we learn the rules of multiplication. One of these rules is that a positive times positive equals positive, a negative times positive equals negative and the slippery one, a negative times negative equals positive. Slippery? Yes, because outside of the mathematics world, mixing a negative with anything, especially another negative can be devastating. Our personal choice of thinking has another mathematic comparison: COMPOUNDING. Regardless of our mental framework (positive or negative), the one we choose sets the direction of our outcomes. My life has proven this repeatedly. When I take a positive path, the outcome is more often positive and with greater intensity. Going negative, more often than not, produces the same compounding but in the negative direction. Being positive does NOT guarantee a successful outcome, but puts the right parts in motion EVERY time. Be positive and surround yourself with positivity in every aspect of your life.

ATTITUDE

ATTITUDE determines our outlook and outcome in life. Good ATTITUDE = Good Outlook and Outcome. Bad ATTITUDE = Bad Outlook and Outcome.

A ttack
T ough
T imes
I ntensely
T enaciously
U sing
D etermination to
E xcel

POSITIVE 1

Two negatives do not make a positive. In life, we must own our **POSI-
TIVE.**

P ut ourselves in a YES mindset
O wn our outcome
S hut out Negative Nellies
I nsist on possibility thinking
T ake charge
I nclude self-encouragement
V erify by visualizing
E liminate doubt

POSITIVE 2 (how)

Experience teaches that living with a **POSITIVE** outlook requires:

P racticing it with purpose
O bstacles treated as springboards
S aying, "Yes, I can" to ourselves often
I nvolving positive people in our lives
T reating setbacks as opportunities
I nserting daily "negative-free" time
V isualizing the outcomes we want
E xpecting the best and working for it

POSITIVE 3 (why)

In life, we can chose to be positive or to be negative. Chose **POSITIVE.**
Why?

P ossibilities are the focus
O pens the mind to potential
S ets the "yes, I can" attitude
I nstills optimism
T ells the mind to "go for it"
I nspires when situations look bleak
V ictory is always in sight
E xpects the best results

BEST and **WORST**

Often the difference between **WORST** and **BEST** performances are driven by our mental state.

"W hat if" is focused on the negative
O nly thinking about "not messing up"
R eally don't believe we can do it
S econd-guessing actions
T alking ourselves out of doing well

B eing in the moment
E xpecting good results
S aying, "I deserve to be here"
T rusting in the preparation

SPARKLE

When joy, love, and compassion are in the heart, an undeniable **SPAR-KLE** is in the eyes.

S ays life is an amazing journey
P uts the joy out for the world to see
A ttracts others with the same spirit
R echarges, revitalizes, refreshes
K eeps smiles easy to come by
L ights up a room by just being there
E xpresses more than what words can

SPARK

One positive thought in the morning can **SPARK** the flame for an incredible day.

S peak
P ositive
A ffirmations
R epeat and
K now it works

SPIRIT

Personal experience convinced me that our **SPIRIT** is contagious. We get what we emit. So,

S et a purpose with purpose
P rotect what we respect
I ntentions must be intentional
R epeat what we want to reinforce
I nspire what we want to ignite
T each what we seek to reach Show true **SPIRIT** always.

ENERGY

ENERGY in every situation is contagious.

E veryone emits their own
N egative or positive, we choose
E very situation thrives on its energy—choose wisely
R egularly check what is being sent
G ets its source from our attitudes
Y ou get what you give in the long run

GLASS HALF FULL

The optimist sees life as a GLASS HALF FULL.

G ets past doubt
L ooks for opportunity
A lways expects the best
S ees the bright side
S omehow smiles regardless

H as a plan
A ccepts reality but fights to improve
L ives for possibilities
F inds a glimmer of hope

F igures out a way
U ses internal strength
L aughs at naysayers
L ets nothing hold them back

DETERMINED

Instead of being detoured by challenges, let's become more determined by them. Instead of being detoured by challenges, let's DETERMINED by them.

D ecide what we want
E mbrace the responsibility
T ake charge
E xpect difficult times
R emain calm
M ake the sacrifices required
I ntensify your purpose
N ever be denied
E mpower ourselves
D edication and determination will prevail

AWAKEN

Each day we can choose to wake up or truly **AWAKEN**.

A rise with a zest for life
W anting to take on the day
A ware it won't be easy
K eep pushing ourselves to yeses
E ncourage ourselves at all times
N ow let's get our coffee and begin

It's a great day to **AWAKEN**!

THOUGHTS

THOUGHTS drive performance, which is based on our actions that are influenced by feelings which come from **THOUGHTS**. We must manage our **THOUGHTS**.

T ake self talk seriously
H ave positive self-conversations
O utlook comes from inner beliefs
U se your TRIGGERS
G ive the mind a positive vision
H ave the courage to believe in yourself
T ell yourself you are prepared
S ay you deserve the outcome you want

UPBEAT

Live each day on the **UPBEAT**.

U sing
P ositive
B ehavior
E very
A ction
T oday!

BLAST

Make today a **BLAST**.

B egin with positive outlook
L ook for opportunities to shine
A llow yourself to experience joy
S how a lift in your step
T ake a little risk today

REWARDING

Finding ways to make work **REWARDING**.

R ejoice in the effort
E ducate as part of the process
W ork because you love it
A lways be committed
R equire there to be fun
D o it for the joy
I nspire yourself
N eutralize challenges with positive attitude
G ive your all and watch what you get

EMISSIONS

We attract what we emit. We must check our **EMISSIONS**.

E xist with positive focus
M ake the best use of our energy
I nsist on the best from ourself
S urround ourself with uplifting people
S ay, "Yes, I Can" when I think I can't
I gnore doubters
O pen our actions to possibilities
N otice incremental positives
S mile early and often

TRIUMPH

Call the day a **TRIUMPH**.

T oday
R eaching
I nside
U sing
M y
P ositive
H ealthy (attitude)

TEMPER

To get through situations of anger, we must learn to temper our **TEMPER**.

T ake a moment and seek calmness
E motions under control
M anage the anger
P eaceful purpose
E liminate blame
R econcile to a common ground

UPLIFTING

Making today an **UPLIFTING** day.

U se
P ositive
L anguage
I nspired
F aith
L ove
I ntensely
N ever
G ive up

HAPPY

Often folks say, "I just want to be **HAPPY**!" Well, here is a start in that direction. Begin by:

H aving
A
P ositive
P erspective
Y 'all

JOYFUL

Today be **JOYFUL**.

J ust
O pen
Y ourself
F or
U plifting
L ove

Being **JOYFUL** also brings Joy to others.

HOPE

It is said **HOPE** is NOT a strategy. Maybe not but **HOPE** is a key foundation to everything.

H ave
O ptimistic
P ositive
E xpectations

BELIEVE

Part of accomplishment and reaching goals is to first BELIEVE in yourself.

B e
E xpectant
L ook
I nside
E nvisioning
V ictory
E verytime

REBOUND

When facing a situation of disappointment, choose to REBOUND.

R elax
E xhale
B e
O ptimistic
U nflappable
D etermined to bounce back

OPPORTUNITIES

Successful people choose to turn setbacks, challenges, and disappointments in life into OPPORTUNITIES and see roadblocks as springboards. What are your OPPORTUNITIES?

O ur
P assionate
P ursuit
O f
R esolving
T o
U se
N ew
I nitiative
T hat
I nspires
E xtraordinary
S uccess

6

UNCONTROLLABLE CIRCUMSTANCES? CONTROL OURSELVES

Most of us need to feel some level of control in our lives. Some are "control freaks." Others are fine with less total control as long as we have a few specific things in our grasp: surroundings, work/life balance, financial comfort, a sense of belonging, etc. It is when our control threshold is out of balance with current circumstance that stress, chaos, and anxiety can roll in with great intensity. My parents taught me the one thing we can always control is how we deal with situations we face. They equated it to needing to play the hand that is dealt or rolling with the punches. The question they taught me to ask myself is: "What CAN I do in this situation to make the most of it?"

CONTROL (two CONTROL freaks)

What can we CONTROL these days? Well, for certain, our thoughts, attitudes, and actions. When I focus on the things I can CONTROL, calmness comes over me.

C are about self and others we love	C ommit
O pportunities emerge from struggle	O urselves
N ow focus on what we can control	N ow
T ake the best actions possible	T aking
R eject asking the WHY question	R esponsibility
O nly focus on "what we CAN do"	O wnership (of our own)
L ive with CONTROL in perspective	L ives

.

ACCEPT 1

If we can't control everything, can we **ACCEPT** this and make the most of the situation?

A llow for this reality
C alm ourselves
C ontrol our emotions
E xplore what we CAN do
P lan our action
T ake appropriate steps

Controlling what we can usually starts within ourselves.

ACCEPT 2

Sometimes we are required to **ACCEPT** the circumstances before we can move beyond them and thrive.

A ll we face is not all our fault
C arefully learn from the situation
C hange only what we can—ourselves
E xpect a challenge and welcome it
P ut our energy to moving forward
T ake control of what we can control

ADJUST

The adjustable wrench is a great invention. It can **ADJUST** to fit the situation at hand. Are we able to **ADJUST**?

A ware we must change to be useful
D etermined to stay relevant
J oyful to be an asset no matter how
U sing our gifts to make things better
S ee adjustments as improvements
T rusting change makes us better

SETBACKS

SETBACKS happen. Moving past them is essential for success.

S ee the big picture
E xamine the facts
T ake responsibility
B egin by forgiving self and others
A ct and do what I need to do
C hallenge myself to do it
K now I will be stronger in the end
S ee myself where I want to be

Thank life for this important lesson.

RESPOND

Ways to RESPOND to adversity.

R each inside and choose to be strong
E xpect it won't be easy
S eek strength through faith
P ut forth your best effort
O ne step at a time
N EVER give up
D etermination is a great companion!

BRIGHT

We can choose to look at the dark or the BRIGHT side of a situation. Try to see both then focus on BRIGHT and move forward.

B eing angry is okay
R esolve to make it better
I mprove by learning the cause
G et past the blame game
H op back into life with more vigor
T ake the lesson and be better

RE-INVENTION

Life seems to require some **RE-INVENTION** every day.

R eally, did that really happen?
E xplain to me what's going on
-
I ncredibly now I have to respond
N ot really expecting that situation
V erified it, so how did it change?
E verything I expected has moved
N ew reality, now I must dig in
T ake charge, and count on myself
I nside strength—feed it and nurture it
O utside strength comes from inside
N ow stay committed to my survival

RE-INVENTION is about growth. No growth = no life!

CRISIS

Dealing with a **CRISIS**? Here is an approach.

C all on your faith
R each deep for inner calmness
I ncubate your confidence
S ee yourself at peace
I nsist you can handle it
S ee it through until the end

BETTER

When life deals a bad hand, we can be Bitter or be **BETTER**. Be BET-TER.

B e the person Grandma thinks we are
E xplore to find opportunity
T ake the lead on improving
T ell the negative to take a walk
E levate the attitude
R eject the victim, be the victor

FIRE

When asked to face the **FIRE** of a difficult situation, answer YES, then jump in.

F irst, everything is not in our control
I nstant heat is not all bad
R espond with all resources (including a sense of humor)
E xpect the unexpected and remember to breathe

IF ONLY

Dealing with the "IF ONLY" factor. Turning it into IT ONLY takes ME.

I t sounds like an excuse
F ocused on blaming others

O wn where you want to be
N ow dedicate yourself to get there
L et NOTHING stop you
Y ou can do ANYTHING you want

CHANGE 1

CHANGE can be great. It is all in our attitude and perspective.

C ircumstances
H appen
A nd
N ew
G reat
E xperiences await

CHANGE 2

Forced or self-induced **CHANGE**, not always pleasant but here is a way to approach it positively.

C ircumstances
H ave
A ltered
N ow
G et
E nergized

CHANGE 3

If you want a better life you must be willing to **CHANGE** it yourself.

C reate your environment
H ave your own dreams
A ct on achieving them
N ever give up
G o the extra mile or two
E xpect the results you dream of

OBSTACLES 1

We all face **OBSTACLES** in life. Here are two ways to look at them.

O ptimists
B elieve
S evere
T roubles
A re
C reated
A s
L essons
E xpanding
S trengths

OBSTACLES 2

It's not how we handle the easy stuff, it's how we handle the **OBSTA-CLES** along the way.

O wn it to remove it
B e ready for some bumps
S tay the course, but accept detours
T ake your time—no rush
A llow for options to develop
C arefully make adjustments
L ead by doing the right thing
E xpect push back
S ay, "No **OBSTACLES** will stop me"

STRUGGLES (2)

We face **STRUGGLES** in life. Some minor, some seem unbeatable. Instead of being dominated by them, take them head on.

S ome	S imply
T imes	T ake
R eality is	R ough
U npleasant	U nexpected
G et our	G litches
G oals in place	G o
L ive and work	L earn
E xpecting new happiness and	E xcel
S uccesses	S ucceed

FRUSTRATION

One certainty in life is we will face and deal with **FRUSTRATION**. One way is to:

F ind
R eassurance
U nder
S tressful
T imes
R emember
A lways
T rust (your)
I nner
O ptimism
N ever (quit)

FRICTION

Sometimes it takes **FRICTION** to get a grip on the important stuff.

F inds the FIGHT in us
R ecognizes a new reality
I nitiates the need for action
C hallenges perspective
T ests what's important
I nstitutes some kind of response
O nly hurts of we don't move with it
N aturally pushes us to "go get 'em"

FRICTION can rub us the **RIGHT** way!

The depths of despair can be like the deep end of a swimming pool. When you have sunk and hit the bottom, where do you have to go but up? Push off the floor with great energy to rise up. Don't let your worst day define you! Make it a launching pad to your intended greatness.

7

DETERMINATION: NAME IT AND CLAIM IT!

Often it is easier to talk ourselves OUT of taking action than it is to go ahead and take a risk. Why? Well, we can simply convince ourselves that if we don't try we can't fail. Or, we conjure up reasons we are not good enough or don't have the time or resources to accomplish our goals. What about the fear of NOT being perfect at first try? I have found that if I want something bad enough—not speaking about material things here—I MUST invoke an unstoppable determination of committing to myself to do whatever it takes to achieve it. This ingredient alone will NOT guarantee success, but without determination to persevere through all the challenges and setbacks, failure is inevitable. IF WE WANT IT, WE MUST STICK WITH IT.

WHY NOT? (a Double "Y NOT")

When striving to achieve a goal and applying yourself to it, sometimes you may feel self-doubt creeping into your thinking. This doubt might question if you will succeed. When this happens, ask yourself a little question: WHY NOT?

W hen
H elping
Y ourself

N othing
O bstructs
T riumph

WHY NOT (the sequel)

When faced with a "why?" situation, ask, "WHY NOT?" Act on it and see what happens.

W hen facing a stressful situation
H ave confidence in yourself
Y ou can if you believe you can

N othing can stop you if you believe
O nly you can limit what you can do
T ake no "no's" as an answer

GUTS

What is meant by "no GUTS, no glory?" When facing a fearful situation and the outcome has been positive, maybe this is GUTS.

G et in there regardless of our fears
U se our capabilities to do our best
T alk to ourselves with positive words
S tay relaxed and let ourselves perform

QUEST

Striving for an important goal often requires treating it as a QUEST.

Q uitting is never an option
U sing all the energy one has
E very ounce of passion
S teady effort over time
T il the goal is reached

WANT TO

Doesn't it seem easier to do the things we WANT TO do vs. things we HAVE to do? Try putting the "WANT TO" attitude on my "HAVE TO" duties.

W ould rather do nothing else
A nxious to get started
N ot to be denied
T oo consumed to be distracted

T aking it head on
O vercoming any obstacle

LIMITS

If we turn off self-limiting doubts, we can set and achieve amazing goals. One way to turn off **LIMITS**.

L et go of self-doubt
I nstill self talk of "Why Not?"
M ake yourself a believer in YOU!
I magine clearly living your dreams
T alk to yourself using "Yes, I Can!"
S ubstitute "I Will" for "I'll Try"

GET UP

Falling is inevitable. To **GET UP** every time is a measure of a successful path.

G ive all you have always
E xpect ups and downs on the way
T ake both in stride

U se your unbridled determination
P ush on toward your goal

BOUNCE

When challenges get in our way, we can be flattened or we can **BOUNCE** back? I'd rather think **BOUNCE** than splat.

B e resilient, frustrate the challenge
O ut work the obstacle
U se our energy on the solution
N ever accept a negative situation
C an do beats want to
E xtend our limits

WISH

How to make a **WISH** come true.

W ork yourself silly
I nsist on your own and others' commitment
S ettle for nothing less than the best
H old on to the dream and do the work

FIGHT (times deux)

Some situations require we **FIGHT** for what we want, especially when we are down. If it's important, dig deep, claim it, and **FIGHT** for the outcome desired!

F orget that you are not winning
I ntensify your intentions
G et focused "in the moment"
H ave awareness and be calm
T ake the situation one step at a time and keep working

Inspiration: Pace Academy Girls Varsity volleyball matches.

FIGHT

If it is important, if it matters to you, if you care about it then **FIGHT** for it!

F ill your fortitude
I nsist on success
G et engaged with the issue
H old on to the end
T ell yourself you are playing to win—repeat!

REACH

Create a habit of continuously striving for goals that at first seem out of **REACH**. One way is to:

R emove mental limits
E xtend possible thinking
A ct expectantly
C reate the habit of stretching
H arbor quiet confidence

WANTING vs. DOING

The difference between **WANTING** something and **DOING** something:

W aiting and hoping
A lthough
N ot
T aking
I nitiative therefore
N ot
G etting where or what you desire

D edicated to
O wning the outcome
I nvesting yourself fully
N ever giving up
G etting where and what you desire

DOUBLE DECLARE

My life has required significant changes several times, i.e. career, relationships, health, etc. One of the steps that has helped drive the change has been to **DECLARE** it.

D ecide what change we want
E ducate ourselves on what it takes
C ommit to achieve the outcome
L et us believe in ourselves
A sk God for guidance and strength
R ecommit if we prefer to quit
E nvision ourselves living the change

I am finding that a key action driving progress to reaching my goals is to **DECLARE** the goal to myself. This action has set things in the right direction.

D evelop clarity of desired outcome
E xpress intentions
C reate a vision of the result
L ive each day focused on my purpose
A ct expectantly
R emember the work must be done
E xpect the outcome I declare

TOMORROW

If we make today our **TOMORROW**, what could we accomplish?

T ackle a goal more intensely
O wn the moment now
M ove with more determination
O rganize and operate at once
R emove procrastination
R ehearse less do more
O ptimize, prioritize, maximize
W hy wait for TOMORROW?

Today is yesterday's **TOMORROW**.

JUMP 1

Often the first action needed for improvement desired is to just **JUMP** in and start.

J ust say you can and you will
U se your mind, heart, and soul
M ake the commitment to action
P rogress each day is the measure

This one came from watching the NBA final last night with a great friend from high school. Thanks Jeff!

JUMP 2

Hesitating on something you want to do? **JUMP** in.

J ust
U se
M ajor
P ositivity!

You can do anything you put your mind and energy on!

OWN IT

If we want to improve our situation, we must believe that we ultimately OWN IT. We own both the opportunity and the responsibility to drive the change we want. We must be willing to name it, claim it, frame it, and develop the determination to sustain it until we realize the change we want.

O bligation is ours
W illing to take responsibility
N o one will do it for us

I t takes our own best effort
T ell ourselves, "Yes"

CONFIDENCE

Here is one way to view and own a life of CONFIDENCE.

C alm
O utlook
N ever ending
F aith
I nspired
D etermination
E ngaging
N ew
C hallenges
E very day

GO FOR IT

To get where you want, you have to GO FOR IT.

G et serious
O wn your situation

F ind your passion
O pen yourself to possibilities
R ecommit to change

I ntensely focus
T ake everything in stride

NO REGRETS

One way to explain living life with **NO REGRETS**.

N ever give up on yourself
O pen your mind to endless possibilities

R each inside of yourself
E ngage with your dreams
G o for your passion
R eject the naysayers
E mbrace the challenges
T rust your heart
S oar like an eagle

LET GO

Moving on, let's **LET GO** of something holding us back. Let's:

L ove
E ach other
T urn off hostilities and

G et
O n with love and compassion

READY

Are you **READY** for the changes you want?

R eally expecting positive
E ngaged in making things happen
A pplying yourself completely
D etermined to do what it takes
"Y es, I can" minded

TERRIFIC

Today will be **TERRIFIC**. Seize it!

T oday
E xpect to
R eceive
R eal
I nsight
F or
I nspiring
C reativity

GREAT

This day will be **GREAT**.

G et
R eady
E xpect
A nother
T errific day

GREATER

This day will be **GREATER**.

G et
R eady
E xpect
A nother
T errific day
E xpect it
R epeat it

AWESOME

Today will be **AWESOME!**

A
W onderful
E xperience
S hall
O verwhelm
M y
E xpectations

INTENSITY

Live **LIFE** with calm **INTENSITY**.

I nvest in yourself
N ow is the time
T ake time to breathe
E xhale to get calm
N ever doubt yourself
S ettle said no successful person, EVER
I mpossible has met its match
T omorrrow is not here, do it now
Y esterday is over, let it go

8

BACK TO THE BASICS:
CHARACTER, VALUES,
AND FAITH

Without a strong foundation, a house will crumble in the face of weather's elements. Without a strong root system, a tree will topple when challenged by the wind. We too must have a strong set of values that define our character. Beliefs and truths are essential tools when facing the challenges of life's journey.

HEART

I believe if we live our life with our **HEART**, our head will put us on the right path.

H arness our true passion
E mbrace it with purpose
A im high, shoot higher
R emember never settle
T rust that determination, effort, and time will get us to our goals

CONTROL

Sometimes it is important to focus on **CONTROL** of one's self.

C hance has a downside
O wn up to the risk
N ow decide what you can lose
T ake your action
R emember your decision
O bey your stance
L et go of temptation

HONOR

To live with **HONOR**.

H elping others as a life commitment
O utrageous selflessness
N ever doubt your passion
O h to live inspired
R eal passion cannot be restrained

INITIATIVE 1

Oh to teach children to take **INITIATIVE** at a young age. 'Tis a lifelong differentiator.

I gnite oneself
N ow is when things get done
I nsist on trying themselves
T ake the first step, then the next
I s first to say, "let me try"
A s curious as a cat
T ell yourself yes when hearing no from others
I s willing to fail but does not care
V iolates the "you can't do that" mantra
E mbraces the challenge

INITIATIVE 2 (another way)

One thing in life ALL successful people take is **INITIATIVE.**

I nsist on starting on your own
N ever wait for a handout
I nspired from within
T ake control and responsibility
I nfuse your passion
A sk for help you will need it
T ake responsibility
I nvite others you need to join you
V alidation will find you
E xcellence follows initiative

SUSTAIN

What does it take to **SUSTAIN** a healthy, positive focus on life?

S tay above the negative messages
U se our strong faith in goodness
S upport the causes that help others
T alk the talk walk the walk ourselves
A llow possibilities to win over doubt
I nsist on "thumbs up" thinking
N urture others to **SUSTAIN** as well

SUSTAINING

Keep at it with a SUSTAINING commitment.

S ure you will prevail
U ndeniable
S teady with the effort
T ake it all in stride
A llow not a single doubt
I ntensify toward the end
N ow one more big push
G reatness is about the long haul

LITTLE THINGS

It's been said ordinary people accomplish great things by doing the LIT-TLE THINGS extraordinarily well. So the LITTLE THINGS matter.

L et no detail go unconsidered
I nspect, inspect, inspect
T ackle things others overlook
T reat everyone with respect
L ook first to help others
E xpect the unexpected

T ake nothing for granted
H ave a backup plan
I nclude those others think don't matter
N ever assume
G o with your gut 95 percent of the time
S eek insight from those closest to the situation

STANDARDS

We get what we will tolerate. If we want to change this we must adjust our STANDARDS.

S tand up for what is right
T reat ourself with respect
A lways do our best
N ever settle for less
D o something new each day
A lways expect the best
R aise our level of effort
D evelop our mind, spirit, and body
S tate our expectations clearly

FRUITFUL

On living a **FRUITFUL** life.

F aith in God
R espect for self and others
U nconditional love
I ndependent thinking
T aking responsibility
F ollowing the heart
U nderstanding and using one's gifts
L iving with passion for helping others

Observed from my father's daily actions.

IMPRESSIVE

One measure of what's **IMPRESSIVE**.

I nterested in others
M otivated always to get better
P ositive about life
R **efuses to give up**
E ager to learn
S ensitive to surroundings
S ees both sides of the story
I s true to their beliefs
V alues values
E xtends a helping hand

HUMILITY

Dominating thought today and living with **HUMILITY**.

H ey, nothing is owed to me
U ntil it's earned, it's not due
M aybe grunt work is the start
I nterviews are about giving, not getting
L et's respect the elders
I f we work, opportunity comes
T alk less and listen more
Y ou get to the top by climbing

STANDARDS

Life requires some sacrifices but never sacrifice our **STANDARDS**.

S tands for
T ruthfulness
A spirations
N urturing instincts
D edication to your goals
A ppetite for knowledge
R espect for self and others
D reams
S elf-esteem

HEART

Been thinking a lot about what it means to have a **HEART**. Have one, open it up to others and give it freely!

H ope—live with it
E xpectation—act with it
A ffirmation—repeat it
R espect—earn it, expect it, and offer it
T rust—don't be afraid to give it

PRIDE

Playing for **PRIDE** vs. the prize.

P utting in your **BEST**
R egardless of the reward
I nspired from within
D oing more than you might want to
E ffort is contagious

STRIVE

Always **STRIVE** to be your best self.

S ee yourself where you want to be
T ell yourself to stick with your effort
R each deep into your heart
I nstruct yourself to keep going
V isualize and verbalize the goal
E xpect the outcome of YES

HUMBLE

On being **HUMBLE**.

H umility above all
U nderstand it takes more than you
M ake sure to thank others
B e appreciative
L isten more than you speak
E ncourage others

SUPER

Being **SUPER** could mean many different things: a terrific athlete, fantastic musician/artist, businessperson, highly skilled mechanic, or crafts person. Well, maybe being **SUPER** means:

S etting
U plifting
P ositive
E xamples
R epeatedly

PREPARE

Want luck? **PREPARE** for it!

P ut forth
R eal
E ffort
P ositive
A ffirmations with
R ealistic
E xpectations

Luck will take care of itself.

CREDIBILITY

A key ingredient to high-quality relationships is credibility.

C onsistent
R eliable
E very
D ay
I n
B usiness
I n
L ife
I ncluding
T o
Y ourself

HIGH ROAD

One way to explain to children about taking the **HIGH ROAD**.

H onesty
I ntegrity
G enerosity
H umility

R espect
O thers
A ccept
D ifferences

CHOICES

Decisions are often about **CHOICES**. All have impact and outcomes. So today involves thinking about the benefits, outcomes, and consequences of the **CHOICES** we make as part of life.

C learly
H ave
O utcomes and
I nvolve
C onsequences in
E very
S ituation

WEALTH

What is real **WEALTH**? Maybe,

W hen
E veryone
A ttains
L ove
T ruth
H appiness

THANKS

Giving **THANKS** is when you:

T ake time and list your blessings
H old the hand of someone you love
A cknowledge your gifts with humility
N otice the beauty around you
K eep your thankful spirit shining
S tay focused on your blessings

ENJOY

Take time to slow down and **ENJOY**.

E xperience the surroundings
N otice the little things
J ust think and be thankful
O bserve without judgement
Y ou might be filled with calmness

PREPARATION

Outcome is often determined by **PREPARATION**.

P utting
R eal
E ffort
P roperly
A llows
R eaching
A chievement
T otally
I ncapacitating
O ne's
N egativity, nervousness, and naysayers

Multiple CHOICES

Life requires we make **CHOICES**. One formula for making them is:

C onsider all factors
H ave and use your values
O pen up to new possibilities
I ntuition—use it
C onsequences—what are they?
E xercise patience
S eek inner peace with the decision

Second CHOICES

Decisions are often about **CHOICES**. All have impact and outcomes. So think about the benefits, outcomes, and consequences of the **CHOICES** we make in life.

C learly
H ave
O utcomes and
I nvolve
C onsequences in
E very
S ituation

HAPPINESS

Make some **HAPPINESS** every day. It will smooth out the rough spots.

H ave
A
P ositive
P erspective
I nsist
N egative
E xits
S ee
S miles

SIMPLIFY

Sometimes just **SIMPLIFY**. When situations seem overwhelming, think **SIMPLIFY**.

S ettle the mind
I nvite calmness
M aintain your positive outlook
P lan actions in large chunks
L et go of self pressure
I nternalize with visualizing the outcome you want
F ocus on the key parts
Y ou'll do the best that you can

SIMPLIFY (again)

To achieve more of what you want, **SIMPLIFY**.

S eek what matters to you
I nvest yourself into what matters
M inimize distractions
P lace your faith in God
L et your gifts guide you
I nsist on loving what you do
F ind a little fun each day
Y ou WILL be the best you can be!

RICHES

Seek a life of **RICHES** more meaningful than any wealth.

R espect, of self and others
I ntegrity
C ompassion
H onesty
E quilibrium (balance)
S implification (back to the basics)

LEARNING 1

Life is a journey of **LEARNING**. Be willing to absorb like a sponge.

L isten to teachers
E xplore new opportunities
A waken to possibilities
R each to farther destinations
N avigate uncharted waters
I nvest in your growth
N ever proclaim MASTERY
G row from every experience

LEARNING 2

Being more interested in what you don't know than what you do know is called a love for **LEARNING**.

L ooking for ways to grow
E nter a room ears open and mouth shut
A cknowledge other's knowledge
R espect those who came before us
N ever expert and always student
I nquiring vs. instructing
N urturing the quest of the unknown
G o forward without fear or risk

LEARNING 3

Always keep **LEARNING**.

L ooking for ways to grow
E xpanding your knowledge base
A pplying yourself
R eading and researching
N ever stop questioning
I nvesting in your learning
N ever closing your mind
G iving your all "in the moment"

TALK LESS, DO MORE

Making a lasting impact, let's **TALK LESS, DO MORE**.

T oday's world
A sks to hear
L ess about what you
K now

L ongs for more
E mpathetic
S incere (involved)
S upport

D edicate
O urselves to

M aking
O urselves
R eally
E ngaged (DOERS)

THANK YOU

If you receive a compliment, respond with two simple words: THANK YOU.

T ake it seriously
H and shake (hug) the compliment giver
A cknowledge with simple a "thank you"
N ever downplay the compliment
K eep smiling and make eye contact

Y our genuine response is enough
O pen your heart and receive it
U se the compliment as encouragement to improve

GENEROUS

In a "what's in it for me?" culture, we can change that by first looking to be GENEROUS.

G ive of yourself first at
E very opportunity
N eeds are
E verywhere
R esults will
O ffer
U nimaginable
S uccesses

LISTEN

It's always a good day to LISTEN more.

L et others do the speaking
I ngest the content
S top! Remember LISTEN
T wo ears, one mouth for a reason
E ase in
N ow to go and learn

FOUNDATION

It takes a strong **FOUNDATION** to support a structure. The same is true in life.

F aith in a loving God
O ptimism and a positive nature
U nconditional love of self and others
N urturing spirit
D edication to striving for greatness
A ttitude of gratitude
T otal commitment to values
I nsistence on honesty
O pen mind and open heart
N ever sacrificing character

VALUES

Teaching a strong **VALUES** system to our children is one of the finest gifts in the world that we can give them.

V ital beliefs system for life
A ttributes for decision-making
L eads and guides our thinking
U nchanging rules of life
E xplains right from wrong
S hows the correct path every time

STUDENT

On becoming a lifelong **STUDENT**.

S eek knowledge aggressively
T ake learning seriously
U se the question "why?" incessantly
D ig for answers intensely
E xercise the mind passionately
N eed to know constantly
T each what you learn freely

Share this with your children and **STUDENT**s. We need to encourage them.

BLESSED

It is easy to help someone feel **BLESSED**. Let them know they are:

B eing
L oved
E very
S ingle
S econd
E very
D ay

BLESSED (doubly)

The only difference between stressed and **BLESSED** is the letters before ESSED. Today say, "I am **BLESSED**" when feeling stressed.

B e calm and feel God's presence
L et go of the can'ts and not's
E mploy your gifts—they are good
S mile knowing you are not alone
S eek help—it is there if you ask
E ngage good expectations
D o this when feeling stressed

MIRACLE

I received mine on April 8, 1961. I came into this world while my mother encountered a dissecting aneurysm of her aorta during labor. I have discussed this medical event with several physicians each who have said neither my mother NOR I should have survived. She lived to be 53. God has blessed me with a family who inspire me every day to be my best. I am the product of a **MIRACLE**—no question!

M ade especially from God's hand
I nstilled with a divine blessing
R eceived a second chance, day ONE
A ccept this gift with uncertainty
C hosen for unknown reasons
L ive each day thankful for God's gift
E mbrace each day with appreciation

HABITS

HABITS are formed from actions we repeat. Studies show it only takes twenty-one days to form a **HABIT**. Habits don't discriminate between good and bad. So we must choose our repeated behaviors carefully. Here is a way to frame thoughts and actions for a desired **HABIT**:

H ealthy for spirit, mind, and body?
A lign actions accordingly and repeat
B ettering or worsening ourselves?
I s this a behavior I want as a habit?
T ake responsibility, desired change
S tick with the good, avoid the bad

GIVING (times two)*

G ets to the root of life's meaning
I nstills joy in the giver
V olunteering is truly priceless
I nvigorates the soul
N o feeling like it
G ets possibilities in focus

Wrote this as I worked in my first Habitat for Humanity event thinking about GIVING.

GIVING**

The bloods flow through the heart better when we are **GIVING**. Feels great.

G ets the soul right
I nspires self and others
V alidates in a soothing way
I nfectious and can spread
N ever gets old
G ets to REAL purpose

Inspired when I was able to give the Pace Academy Arts Alliance Members the gift of Annie Sellick's beautiful music (April, 2013).

ANGEL

Be someone's **ANGEL** today.

A ct with a helping hand
N otice an opportunity to nurture
G ive upon seeing the chance
E xpect nothing in return
L ift up someone in need

FAITH

We all have times in our lives when hurt, pain, doubt, and sadness seems to consume us. These are the times that test and should strengthen our **FAITH**.

F or
A ll
I n
T ime
H eals

PRAYER

When facing a test where you have to be strong yet the results are out of your control, why not put it to **PRAYER**?

P ut it in God's hands
R ely on his promise and love
A sk for strength and faith
Y es we are human, but He is not
E mbrace that all is in His control
R est in knowing you are not alone

GIFTS (many)

We all have **GIFTS**.

G od-given talents intended for
I nspirational acts
F or self and others
T reated with great care
S hared with abandon

Inventory them and let's use them to the maximum.

GIFTS

Everyone has unique talents, especially talents that can help others. And by using these talents in that way, the joyful rewards are immeasurable. These talents are called GIFTS.

G od
I nstalled
F eatures
T o
S hare

Use them, share them, and we are all better off.

MEANINGFUL

Make everything you do in life MEANINGFUL.

M ake
E very
A dventure
N ew
I nteresting
N atural
G o
F or
U nimaginable
L evels of happiness

RISEN

My father taught me by example to speak quietly about my faith and to just live it. So on this Easter Day, I simply say RISEN! (written March 31, 2013)

R ejoicing in His unconditional love
I nspired to share my faith through actions
S acrificed His life so we might live
E nriched with His blessings
N ever doubting He has a plan for me

9

YOU NIQUE: THANK GOD NO ONE IS LIKE YOU!

The concept of the "Popularity Contest" is hard to eliminate. Especially in the fast-paced, "image is everything" world of today. Please take pause and know that God created every person with unique gifts, talents, and purpose. Take a moment each day to celebrate your uniqueness. For these qualities make you the amazing gift you are.

UNIQUE

U nderstand YOU ROCK!
N otice the nuances—they make you special
I nternalize your uniqueness is a gift
Q uick high five yourself
U R amazing—deal with it
E mbrace the DIFFERENCE

BE YOURSELF

For today **BE YOURSELF**, then repeat daily:

B elieve you are unique
E mbrace your gifts

Y ou are beautiful
O ffer your spirit
U se your energy
R espect yourself
S ee possibilities
E xpect the best
L ive life as a blessing
F orgive, forget, and forge onward

BE YOU

When the world seems to challenge who you are, the best move is to simply **BE YOU**.

B e your best
E njoy your uniqueness

Y ield not to unwanted influences
O kay, now move on!
U se your gifts—no one else has them Here's to you being you!

TREASURE

Everyone has unique life experiences. We chose to call it baggage or our **TREASURE** chest.

T eaches us life lessons
R eminds us or our influences
E xplains our point of view
A llows us to FEEL emotions
S hould give us perspective
U se it to improve and grow
R each into it for understanding
E mbrace every **TREASURE**

MOVES

What **MOVES** you?

M akes you dive into life
O pens your spirit
V alidates you
E levates your passion
S timulates your soul

Relentlessly do what **MOVES** you!

INDIVIDUAL

Thank God no one else is like you. You are an **INDIVIDUAL** and bring unique gifts to improve this world.

I n a league of your own
N ot like ANYONE else
D ivinely created for great things
I ntended to achieve
V aluable "as is"
I nfectious when you smile
D estined to make a difference
U nique with priceless gifts
A wesome as you are
L imitless if you believe in yourself

CELEBRATE

Remember to **CELEBRATE** yourself often.

C hallenge yourself
E ncourage yourself
L ove yourself
E mbrace yourself
B e yourself
R espect yourself
A spire yourself
T rust yourself
E levate yourself

AMAZING

Life is **AMAZING** when we stop trying to amaze others.

A llow our uniqueness to be strong
M ake the world we want emerge
A ccept what comes with being ourselves
Z oom into what matters inside
I nsist on picking positive
N otice the little goodness
G o in the direction of the heart

EQUITY

Cherish your personal **EQUITY**. It is your gift and why you are here!

E veryone is gifted
Q uench your thirst for life with it
U se your EQUITY and give it to others
I nvest in what you CAN do
T alk about it less and use it more
Y ou are unique and the world needs you

GIFTS (abound)

We all have **GIFTS**.

G od-given talents intended for
I nspirational acts
F or self and others
T reated with great care
S hared with abandon

Inventory yours and let's use them to the maximum.

BEAUTIFUL

A **BEAUTIFUL** person.

B rings
E nthusiastic
A ttitude
U nselfish
T eam
I nspiration
F ull of
U nconditional
L ove

These are all choices and visible only through actions.

WEIRD

What is different about us makes us unique and beautiful? This lesson takes time to learn. Kids call being different "**WEIRD**." But WEIRD is:

W hen
E veryone's
I ndividuality
R eveals
D istinction

DIFFERENCE

You are DIFFERENT, so make a **DIFFERENCE.**

D iscover your gifts relentlessly
I nsist on being true to yourself
F ind your GO zone
F ocus to master your uniqueness
E xercise your passion
R ejoice that you are unique
E nergize and execute
N avigate with your own compass
C ollaborate with other unique people
E xpect your gifts to make an impact

*Obstacles that we face in life
can pose two questions:*

*Why me? (the Victim)
or
Why NOT me? (the Victor)*

*Choose to be the Victor you were
born to be and watch the
obstacles vanish.*

10

ONE DAY AT A TIME:
DAYS OF THE WEEK

The cycle of days repeat one time in seven. We certainly have our favorites: weekends, paydays, three-day weekends, right? Well, if we need a way to energize regardless of what day it is? Here are ways to look at each day.

SUNDAY

S uper
U plifting
N ew
D ay
A men
Y 'all

MONDAY

M ove
O ut
N egative
D eliver
A mazing
Y eses!

TUESDAY

T oday
U se
E xtra
S trong
D edication
A ttacking
Y our goals

HUMPDAYS or WEDNESDAY

H olding
U r
M ind
P ositive
D ramatically
A dvances
Y our
S ituation

W hen
E veryone
D oubts
N ever
E ver
S top your
D edication
A lways do
Y our best

THURSDAY

T hink
H ow
U
R
S ucceeding
D aily
A ffirming
Y ourself

FRIDAY message TGIF

If life becomes too much to handle,

T rust
G od
I n
F aith

SATURDAY

S trongly
A ffirm
T hat
U
R eally
D eserve
A ccomplishment
Y es

WORD FOR THE MONTH CLUB:
REUSE EACH MONTH

E very month in a year gives us a symbolic step on the stairs to achievement. Breaking a year down to twelve segments can provide digestible pieces to measure progress to goals, adjust our targets, and celebrate incremental successes. Here is a word for each month to spark a little "get after it" inspiration.

JANUARY

It begins with **JANUARY**.

J ust
A dd
N atural
U plifting
A ttitude and the
R esults will come
Y es, they will

FEBRUARY

FEBRUARY can easily be a dreary month. Say NO to Dreary and YES to DOING!

F acilitate
E nergy and
B ounty
R echarging yourself and others
U plifting
A ll you encounter
R esulting in
"Y es, I can" attitudes

MARCH

Let's celebrate the month of **MARCH** (my mother's birth month). She taught me:

M aking dreams come true takes commitment
A pplying myself is critical
R each a little farther each day
C hallenge myself to do everything it takes
H ave faith that doing these things will get me where I want
    to be

APRIL

The season begins to change. Gardens show determination to emerge in their full glory.

A time to become stronger and more determined
P erfect opportunity to blossom
R ecommit to growth
I nspired to be alive
L iving every day to its fullest

MAY

Setting the tone for a fabulous month!

M ake your dream happen!
A pply yourself and say NO to negatives
Y ou can accomplish anything you want

JUNE

Moving into **JUNE** means:

J oyful living
U nselfish giving
N ever quiting
E ver growing

JULY

For the month of JULY:

J ump in and set your own goals
U se all your energy and determination
L et go of self-imposed limits
Y ou can accomplish anything

AUGUST

When it's AUGUST:

A lways
U sing
G od's given
U nique
S trengths and
T alents

SEPTEMBER

SEPTEMBER is a time of beginnings.

S et our intentions for the approaching Fall
E merging crispness in the air
P ut our purpose in focus for the last quarter of the year
T ake a moment to appreciate the summer times
E njoy the turn of the season
M ake the most of our labors
B etter our efforts each day
E ncourage learning as the school year starts
R outines can change so stay calm

OCTOBER

Hello, OCTOBER.

O pportunities
C oming
T o
O ffer
B right
E xciting
R ewards

NOVEMBER

It's **NOVEMBER** and the holiday season is often difficult for many. Here is a way to approach it.

N ew
O pportunities
V erified
E veryday
M ust
B e
E xpectant and
R eady

DECEMBER

One twelfth of life takes place in **DECEMBER**. Tackle **DECEMBER** with:

D edication
E nthusiasm
C ommitment
E ffort
M otivation
B enevolence
E nergy
R esourcefulness

WHEN THE BATTERIES
ARE LOW: RECHARGE

Inspiration can come from anywhere, including parents, a coach or teacher, a book, a movie, a success story, a sunrise or sunset, and many other surprising sources. But after the initial flame tries to fade, it is up us as individuals to foster the desire and recognize when we need to stoke the fire and rekindle the passion. When the batteries get low, here are a few ideas to recharge.

RECHARGE

We all feel drained at times. Some ways to **RECHARGE**:

R est
E xercise—it's an energy source
C all an old friend and laugh
H ydrate, drink lots of water
A void negative energy drainers
R eprioritize what's important now
G ood food choices
E mpower yourself with positivity

RECHARGE (again)

Does a day go by without us ensuring we **RECHARGE** our cell phone? But we often go forever without recharging ourselves. Kind of silly, right?

R egularly
E xhale
C lear your
H ead
A nd
R efocus
G oals
E xpectations

BOOST

What can we do when we need a BOOST?

B egin by letting go of the negative
O pen the mind to possibilities
O wn the responsibility to self-boost
S et targets that are reachable
T ell ourselves "we can if we want" Repeat as needed.

PLAY

I was reminded one night that it is SO important to **PLAY** a little each day.

P ut life's struggles aside
L etting ourselves escape for a time
A llowing ourselves to just "BE"
Y ou, we all, can use a moment away

Make time to **PLAY.**

LAUGH

A good **LAUGH** can change our outlook in an instant.

L ook at some of life's little annoyances as funny
A llow your mind and body to find the humor
U se the power of a laugh to release some stress
G et a good chuckle as often as possible
H ealing is a laugh's secret outcome

MUSIC

MUSIC is VITAL to life!

M anifests
U ncontrollable
S miles
I nstills
C orrectness about the world—calmness, confidence, courage—you
   pick your own C word.

Listen to some TODAY and everyday. Make a commitment to see and hear it LIVE!

SLOW DOWN

SLOW DOWN when haste looks like the only option:

S top and pay attention
L ook at the alternatives
O bserve with calmness
W ait with patience

D oing this
O pens possibilities
W hen rushing
N ever reveals them

THOUGHTS (a couple of them)

Being alone with our THOUGHTS is a time that highly influences how we perceive ourselves. When I am focusing on how I use that time and what I say to myself, I find these moments powerful.

T alk with encouragement at all times
H ave some self humor
O nly we control self-talk
U se time to rebuild NOT tear down
G ive yourself some credit
H ave belief in yourself
T ake time to love yourself
S ee yourself as your own coach

THOUGHTS drive performance, which is based on actions that are influenced by feelings, which come from THOUGHTS. We must manage our THOUGHTS.

T ake self-talk seriously
H ave positive self-conversations
O utlook comes from inner beliefs
U se your TRIGGER
G ive the mind a positive vision
H ave the courage to believe in yourself
T ell yourself you are prepared
S ay you deserve the outcome you want

CHUCKLE

Do you ever see someone just laughing or with a smile for no apparent reason and wonder what is so funny? I find that laughing a little each day helps lighten some of life's seemingly serious pressures. Find time today to **CHUCKLE**.

C hose to laugh a little each day
H umor releases stress
U nleashes creativity
C hallenges the perceived reality
K ills tension for a short while
L inks us to others (it's universal)
E ngages the mind with possibilities

FORTIFY

Strength from within to make ourselves stronger is to **FORTIFY**.

F ind a source of energy
O btain a calm inner state
R each deep to gather resolve
T ake moment and focus
I ntensify the desire
F ire when ready
Y es is the mantra

EMERGE

It's not how you submerge but how you **EMERGE** that matters.

E ngage the determination
M ake the choice to be victorious
E nergize the will to survive
R each deep...no DEEPER.
G ive it EVERYTHING you have
E levate, escalate, and exhilarate

MELODY

Thinking about **MELODY** as a natural part of life. A good **MELODY** is like a good life.

M akes the heart pound freely
E levates possibility thinking
L ifts positive spirits to new heights
O pens up to what we are open to
D rives us to our passion
Y ells, "Go for it!"

FOR YOU

Make time today FOR YOU.

F ind some time and a place today
O kay, now escape for a moment
R eflect on something you cherish

Y ou deserve a short escape
O nly focused on you
U se these moments to strengthen

SETTLED

Thinking about achieving a SETTLED mind as a step to a calm, clear problem-solving approach.

S implify the situation
E xhale deeply and often
T ake what's huge and break it down
T ackle smaller pieces with focus
L isten and adjust as required
E xhale again
D ecide and believe it's doable this way

ROTATE

Farmers ROTATE their crops to ensure the soil's nutrients are replenished. What should we ROTATE to keep replenishing our mind, heart, and soul?

R ead a book at least every ninety days
O bserve something usually taken for granted and learn from it
T ry a new way to energize ourselves
A sk why? of one long standing habit
T each ourselves a new skill
E njoy the change

What do you suggest?

SURROUND

SURROUND yourself with what makes you happy.

S eek your JOY
U se your gut
R efuse to settle
R efreshing and revitalizing
O wn the space
U nleash your spirit
N ow is the time
D o it for yourself

DAYDREAM

Turning a **DAYDREAM** into a dream come true.

D ream
A nything
Y ou want
D edicate yourself to achieving the dream
R ealize the work will be hard
E xpect highs and lows
A ccept no substitutes
M ake it happen for yourself

CHEER

Sometimes you just have to **CHEER** for yourself, especially when you feel no one else is.

C auses yourself to believe in YOU
H elps us take our own responsibility
E liminates "pleasing others" motives
E nables self-love and determination
R elying on yourself attracts others

Today start by CHEERing yourself on!

SPACE

There are times when everyone needs their own **SPACE** to find their best place. Make time for your own **SPACE**.

S pecial place mental or physical
P lace to connect to your core self
A llows a way to unplug for a while
C hallenges you to dump distractions
E nables you to return refreshed

What is your **SPACE**?

For me? In the garden, behind the drums, or playing any sport.

GARDEN

Advice to my girls? Always have a **GARDEN**.

G et into the dirt—it gets into the soul
A ccomplishes things work life can't
R ejuvenates everything
D elivers us from stress
E nriches the spirit
N urtures the nurturer

TWIST

Sometimes it just takes a new angle to see our opportunities in a new way. Try making a simple **TWIST**.

T ake a step back and a quick pause
W iden the focus of the mind's eye
I nspect what has been omitted
S pin the point of view
T ake a breath and reengage

LIGTHGEN UP

We often take ourselves too seriously. It is important sometimes to just **LIGHTEN UP**.

L et go for a minute
I nstead just laugh
G ive yourself a break
H ave a carefree moment
T ake a load off your mind
E scape the pressure
N ow reengage

U se you new perspective
P roceed to new heights

STUCK

Ever feel **STUCK** with where you are in life? Try this:

S tart and commit to a new activity
T reat yourself as #1 for thirty minutes every day
U nplug the unproductive routines, replace with productive ones
C hallenge yourself to make small, steady changes
K eep track of progress and never give up

FRESH

Work to stay **FRESH**.

F ind new ways to do things
R elease negative anchors
E stablish one new healthy habit
S hare a courteous act
H andle life with optimism

REFRESH

New school year, renewed client connections, new job starting today?
Whatever is in your day **REFRESH** it today.

R each out with energy
E ngage like you mean it
F ocus on the moment
R elish the opportunity
E xpect a good outcome
S hare a kind word
H ave a GREAT Day

HUMOR

Make time in you day for **HUMOR**.

H aving
U ncontrollable
M oments
O f
R elease by laughing

Try it! You will feel better!

SMILE

A midday inspiration can be as simple as a **SMILE**.

S haring
M usic
I nspires
L ife's
E xcitement

GIGGLE

Sometimes, we take myself and life situations too seriously. This morning the word **GIGGLE** surfaced to my mind. Yes, there are serious situations we all face. Maybe they can lighten a little if we find some time to **GIGGLE**.

G et
I ntensely
G ood
G ut
L aughter
E veryday Try it today.

PATIENCE

Sometimes we need...wait for it... **PATIENCE**.

P ush the pause button
A ccept that time is your friend
T ake a break
I nhale deeply, deeper
E xhale long and slowly
N ow refocus
C alm the mind
E xpect the best with no time limit

CALM

Intentionally find some **CALM** time each day to control and own your emotions.

C reate
A
L ittle
M oment for yourself

CALMNESS

In times of CHAOS, seek **CALMNESS**.

C onfidence from within
A ffirmation of outcome
L oving heart
M editative moments
N ever quit mentality
E ven keel of emotion
S trength from God
S ense of imminent victory

BREAK (or 2)

Give yourself a **BREAK** to:

B e thankful for your blessings
R eflect on the passing year
E njoy the time with family
A lways believe in yourself
K now your commitment and hard work pays off

BREAK

We are often the hardest on ourselves. We all need a **BREAK** now and then. Take one and

B reathe deeply
R elax intently
E scape the perceived intensity
A llow you mind to calm itself
K eep things in perspective

STRONG LIKE A BULL: STRENGTH, DEDICATION, AND COMMITMENT

Strength can be physical, mental, emotional, spiritual, etc. One characteristic of all strengths is they must be exercised to be maintained and to expand. Staying strong requires dedication, commitment, and repetition. Strength of purpose requires mental persistence and focus when often it is easier to be distracted. Promising ourselves and believing we owe it to ourselves to stay focused keeps us moving in the right direction.

STRONG (several ways)

Today, believe in yourself and stay **STRONG**. You will succeed.

S tand
T all
R emain
O ptimistic
N ow
G o for it

When facing a seemingly insurmountable challenge, find one thing you feel **STRONG** about: your faith, your determination, your confidence, your willingness to try, your unwillingness to sit and do nothing. By feeling **STRONG** in some small way, you start seeing possibilities.

STRONG

S tart believing in you, not the challenge
T hink of your source of strength
R ely on this strength to get started
O vercome doubt, lead with your strength
N ow do what you can today, tomorrow repeat
G ive your all using your strength

STRONG

One thing every dad should teach his daughters. Be **STRONG**.

S elf-reliance pays for itself
T ake compliments with sincerity, but not too seriously
R espect your mind AND body
O wn providing for yourself
N urture others who never heard this from their dads
G row always from the inside out

STRONG

Remember you are **STRONG** if you:

S ee yourself improving
T ackle your situation with optimism
R each for more than you think possible
O utwork the desire to quit
N avigate with calmness
G ive yourself credit

STRENGTH 1

We all have inner **STRENGTH**. Tap into yours today and believe you have it. Be:

S trong
T hrough
R ough
E vents
N o doubts
G etting
T here
H umbly

STRENGTH 2

STRENGTH is not an end result but something we grow incrementally each day.

S eries of small daily improvements
T rust in the process
R einforce the outcome desired
E xpect what you work for
N ow get on with it
G et closer to your goal each day
T reat yourself with love and respect
H ave belief you will get there

BRAVE 1

The best learning happens outside your comfort zone. Accept this and be **BRAVE.**

B e calm and in the moment
R ealize the discomfort will pass
A llow your mind to open to potential
V alue past similar experiences
E xhale and absorb the newness

BRAVE 2

Be **BRAVE.**

B elieve in yourself
R ely on yourself
A dvocate for yourself
V ictory, victory, and victory
E xcel, excel, and excel

BRAVERY 1

Staying focused on the goal at hand and paying no attention to the dangers lurking while attaining it.

B eing committed to the cause
R eaching with confidence
A ligned only with the mission
V ested in the desired outcome
E liminate doubting thoughts
R egardless, you are ALL IN
Y eilding to no obstacles

BRAVERY 2 (again)

I see inspiring **BRAVERY** everyday. Friends fighting illness, relationship struggles, financial hardships, and so on. What is the common thread?

B elieve in you when all by yourself
R ealize the risk yet act anyway
A ttack the situation with your ALL
V oices say, "Yes, I can regardless."
E xtend actions beyond your beliefs
R ely on instinct rather than intellect
Y ou do what you have to do

RESILIENT

On being **RESILIENT**...

R efuse to give up
E ven when it would be easy to quit
S aying to yourself, "keep going"
I nsisting on seeing it to the end
L etting go of any doubt
I nstead believing in yourself
E nduring to earn the reward
N othing but positive effort
T aking on every obstacle

RESILIENCE

One measuring stick I see used by successful people is **RESILIENCE**. It's not about the number of failed attempts, but about the number of times one gets back up and keeps going. Today show **RESILIENCE**.

R equires reaching deep within
E specially after a disappointing result
S aying, "I will not be defeated."
I n spite of how things might look
L etting no one discourage me
I nsisting on moving on
E mpowered by unwavering desire to achieve
N ever giving up
C hallenging myself beyond my belief
E xpecting better outcomes with each additional effort

FIGHT

If it is important, if it matters to you, if you care about it, then **FIGHT** for it!

F ill your fortitude
I nsist on success
G et engaged with the issue
H old on to the end
T ell yourself you are playing to win, repeat!

RESPOND

Our strength is tested and revealed when we must **RESPOND** to adversity.

R ealize adversity is part of life
E xpect some difficult times
S ay to yourself, "I've got this"
P romise yourself to be strong
O wn your thoughts and feelings
N ow face adversity head on
D edicate yourself to being positive

TENACITY

Today's focus: **TENACITY**.

T ake
E very
N egative
A wful
C ircumstance
I nvert
T o
Y ES

COMMIT

One of the first steps to reaching our goals is to **COMMIT** ourselves. Yes, we all need help to achieve our goals, but first we must **COMMIT** ourselves to the goal and to the work it will take. GO FOR IT!

C ount
O n
M e
M aking
I t
T here

WILLPOWER 1

WILLPOWER means...

W hen you want to give up
I nside you must view
L ook for the strength
L et's get up and let's DO
P ut in the extra effort
O f more than the rest
W hen others give up
E xtra effort yields the best
R efuse to quit

WILLPOWER 2 (said another way)

Achieving something worthwhile in life requires **WILLPOWER**.

W anting to achieve a goal
I nterruptions will abound
L ock in your focus
L et nothing distract you
P repare for potential setbacks
O wn your emotions
W ork hard
E njoy the process
R esults will come

SUSTAINING

Sometimes a key to winning the battle is staying in it and **SUSTAINING** your commitment and effort.

S teady
U nyielding
S acrifice
T o
A chievement
I ncluding
N ever
G iving up

BELIEVE 1

To achieve your goals, it is vital to BELIEVE you can and will reach them. A simple strategy to help is to visualize your success in your mind FIRST. See yourself in your mind's eye with the achievement of the goal. Do this early and often. Seeing your success before achieving it helps to:

B egin
E verything
L ooking
I nside
E very time
V isualize
E xcellence

BELIEVE 2 (some more) BELIEVE in yourself.

B egin by believing you can
E xpect to work hard
L earn and apply the knowledge
I nsist that you persist
E ncourage yourself when really down
V oices in your head must be positive
E ffort expands when self-belief is high

GREATNESS

GREATNESS is attained by the journey, not the outcome.

G oing beyond perceived limits
R ealizing the work will be harder than you imagined and enjoying it
E xpecting adversity and embracing it
A ffirmation of wanting the change you are seeking
T aking responsibility of the situation
"N ever, ever give up" attitude
E ndless focus on your intentions
S ettling for only the best
S trong amount of humility

Go be GREAT!

STRIDE 1 (or strides)

Take things in **STRIDE**.

S tay true to your dreams
T ackle challenges with unyielding effort
R id yourself of doubt
I nject your will
D ecide, dedicate, and do
E xpect struggles, work for success

Taking today in **STRIDE**.

STRIDE 2

My parents advised me to take things in life in **STRIDE**.

S tay steady with my effort
T ake setbacks as opportuities for adjustments
R edouble my commitment
I nspiration drives energy; stay inspired
D elight in the journey
E nter all new opportunities this way, i.e. repeat the above

TOUGH 1

What does it mean to be **TOUGH**?

T ake on responsibility
O ut work everyone
U nrelenting effort
G iving 100 percent
H elp others reach their destinations

TOUGH 2 (another way)

When you are in any **TOUGH** situation, try this approach.

T rust in yourself
O wn your actions
U nderstand the options and outcomes
G et help—you will need it
H ave faith and work hard

This approach has helped me many times. I continue to go to it often.

SHARP

Keeping **SHARP** skills is a key to growth. If you're not growing, you are backing up. Stay **SHARP**.

S teady quest to improve
H aving dreams and goals in sight
A lways challenged to be better
R efusing the status quo
P ositive outlook always

SHARPER

Not every day can be sharp. If today was one of those days that make you appreciate the good ones, tomorrow you can be **SHARPER**.

S tart with thanks for my blessings
H andle with joy and positive outlook
A ttune to possibilities
R efocus on what's important
P repare to face challenges
E ager to solve problems
R ely on faith—God is with you

REINFORCE

Whatever we choose to **REINFORCE** gets stronger. Let's make wise choices.

R espect for self and others
E xpect the outcomes we work for
I nvest in improving our lives
N urture our surroundings
F ocus on making a contribution
O pen our hearts and minds
R eserve judgement
C hoose the high road every time
E ngage in everyday with passion

What will you REINFORCE today?

DECISIONS

Love your **DECISIONS**.

D ecide what's important
E liminate the naysayers
C omit to doing what it takes
S et little goals on the way
I gnore the urge to quit
O wn the process and outlook
N avigate with positive thoughts
S ettle for nothing short of the goal

PERFORMANCE

Whenever I have performed well at something I can point to some specific ingredients which aided the performance. I have found maximizing **PERFORMANCE** for me takes:

P reparation—no substitute
E xcitement about being there
R eminding myself I am ready
F ocus on a mentally and physical relaxed state
O btaining a rhythm of deep breathing
R epeatedly rehearse in my mind a successful performance
M oving with purpose
A cting with an internal confidence
N ow trusting myself
C almness in the moment
E xpecting the desired outcome, let go and PERFORM

ALL IN

The gambling bet "**ALL IN**" often connotes taking the risk of losing everything. Begging the question "is **ALL IN** a wise move?" In life, accomplishing our goals and dreams to their fullest, requires being **ALL IN** with our personal commitment. This in fact increases the likelihood of success. Life's ironies.

With life, let's get **ALL IN**.

A llocate all we have to our goals
L ive committed to goal achieving
L etting go of fear of failure

I nsist on self-commitment and belief
N othing will hinder achievement

BLOSSOM

The gardens are emerging from dormancy one day at a time. As we work on our own changes, have the patience to let them **BLOSSOM**.

B e faithful that the work will pay off
L ook at growth as often incremental
O bserve the process vs. the outcome
S ee the beauty in small changes
S ee yourself improving daily
O pen up to what nourishes you
M ake each day in some way special

ONE YEAR

It is almost **ONE YEAR** of my writing a daily motivational message. The writing journey has molded me in many ways and taught me so much.

O pened my mind to possibilities
N ew outlook developed
E ver stronger, ever grateful

"Y es, I can"—still my favorite words
E xpect good things and they happen
A lways work hard
R each further than you can imagine

FORGET

FOR us to GET where we want, sometimes we have to **FORGET** where we have been and move on.

F ind the good and release the rest
O pen up to the possibilities
R each for your life's steering wheel
G o in the direction of growth
E xpect it to hurt a little on the way
T rust your heart, let it lead

PROGRESS

"One Mailbox at a Time." Conquering a huge goal might best be tackled with consistent incremental **PROGRESS**. Think savings, fitness, skills development etc. I had never run before. When I started training, I was frustrated I couldn't go very far before tiring. I decided to set a goal to run the distances between mailboxes and told myself, "Just one more mailbox, just one more mailbox." In a few weeks, I was running further with more ease than ever.

P ragmatically
R ehearsing
O urselves
G aining
R esults
E xpecting
S teady
S uccesses

So instead of finding frustration in the distance between you and your goal, seek **PROGRESS** toward it every day.

TRY AGAIN

If at first you don't succeed, **TRY AGAIN**.

T otally
R espect
Y ourself

A lways
G ive
A bsolutely
I ntensely
N ever quit

DRIVEN 1

To accomplish what YOU want, you must be **DRIVEN** from the inside.

D edication
R espect
I ntensity
V igor
E ffort
N ever quit

DRIVEN 2

For a friend who asked me for a way to instill in his work team the need to be **DRIVEN**. Hope this helped! To accomplish our targets and goals, we must be **DRIVEN**.

D edicated to the task
R espectful of the process
I ntense with purpose
V igorously determined
E ngaged with commitment
N ever giving up

More HARD WORK

We have all been told it takes **HARD WORK** to accomplish our goals. What does that mean?

H ave a positive framework
A sk for help
R eally focus
D edicate yourself

W elcome advice
O pen your heart and mind
R efuse to settle
K eep smiling

When you come upon stumbling blocks, see them as stepping stones. Circumstances are what we make them. Choose to make the most of them.

14

ACTIONS ARE LOUDER THAN WORDS: IMPACT ON OTHERS

What we say, what we do, what we don't say and don't do all have an influence on others. Our actions do speak louder than our words. Actions as simple as a thoughtful nod, a quiet "that a girl," or an encouraging pat on the back can change someone's day, week, or complete outlook. An unknown side effect of our actions is that often we may never directly know the impact they have on others. So, why not look for opportunities to offer positive nuggets to others?

COURTESY
When I have experienced even small acts of **COURTESY**, received or given, I get a sense of goodness in the world.

C ould change a life or two
O utreach a hand to GIVE, not get
U plifts the spirit
R equests nothing in return
T akes just a little conscious effort
E stablishes a human connection
S ome situations it's not easy
Y ou might just feel good about it

WARMTH
WARMTH can come from a blanket, a meal, a smile, an outreached hand, a hug, and anything else the helps others. WARMTH seems to be something we get as soon as we give it.

W e should
A lways
R each out
M aking every effort
T o
H elp others

LEGACY
Everyone on earth leaves his or her own **LEGACY**. I have thought about what I want mine to be. How about you?

L eft the world a better place than I found it
E ncouraged others along the way
G ave before asking
A dvocated and lived with personal responsibility
C ultivated seeds of optimism and passion in others
"Y ES, I CAN" was etched in the mind of every child I encountered

ATTRACTIVE
I have been thinking about what is **ATTRACTIVE** to me and has led to the great relationships in my life. What I have found **ATTRACTIVE** in great people is below. Yours?

A ware of others first
T alking less than listening
T aking less than giving
R especting self and others
A ccepting, not rejecting
C onfident, never cocky
T eacher more than teller
I nterested more in others
V alues more than valuables
E xcited more than exciting

BEING THERE
In my times of greatest need, the best gifts I have received have come from friends just **BEING THERE**. Sometimes that's all it takes.

B eing a pillar of support
E mpathy without unrequested advice
I t's about PRESENCE, not presents
N urturing by actions
G iving without asking

T alking less, listening more
H elping when it seems helpless
E ngaging in an energy exchange
R especting vs. rejecting
E xpecting nothing in return

HUGS
The best home remedy for any ailment is **HUGS**.

H elps show love and care without words
U seless unless or until given
G ives protection and comfort
S eems to help the giver too
Give some **HUGS** every day.

More HUGS
The feeling of a strong and meaningful embrace: **HUGS**. When given away the "get" is better than the "give."

H eaven's
U niversal
G ift
S haring LOVE

SERVICE
Live a life of **SERVICE** to others.

S eek opportunities to serve
E mpower the powerless
R each out as far as you can
V isualize, verbalize, and mobilize
I mprove the lives of others
C hallenge yourself to do more
E ncourage others by your actions

SERVICE (again)
I have been fortunate to be around many folks who have always put others first. They seemed to experience such joy through a life of **SERVICE**.

S omething only for others
E xtend a nonrepayable gift
R espectful of the receiver
V isibility of the act NOT required
I ncreases the giver's joy
C hanges a life instantly
E mpowers the belief in goodness

Let's do one act today focused on **SERVICE** to others, then repeat!

EMPATHY
Is it possible to see a person's opposite opinion or position without judging or rejecting them as a person? EMPATHY is what my parents called it.

E xtend an open mind
M ake extra effort to listen
P ut yourself in others' shoes
A lign with their situation
T ake away judgement
H ave understanding instead
Y ou can make a difference

ADVICE
ADVICE can be an amazing gift to be given and taken with humility if the giver is:

A lways thinking of others
D elivered with care and compassion
V aluable in content and context
I ntended to teach and learn
C hoose the time and place
E xpressed always with LOVE

FIT IN
When seeking to help others, we can often be stifled, not knowing what to do. Here is a simple action phrase to overcome the hesitation: Get in where you FIT IN!

F ind the need you can serve
I nside your heart you will know
T ake initiative and act

I t can be the small, but it will matter
N ow see how easy that is?

GIVE
GIVE before you get. Things always work out better that way.

G et involved, vastly energizing
I ntense and very exciting
V ictory emerges
E mpowering

ATTENTIVE
I seem to learn more and have more meaningful interactions when actively **ATTENTIVE**.

A ware of others in the surroundings
T ake focus off of self
T ake time to be truly interested
E nergize others and self by tuning in
N otice without being reminded
T ake initiative to help
I nvolved with purpose
V iscerally engaged
E ncouraging and encouraged

CHARITY
Finding a way to help others every day, **CHARITY**.

C ount our blessings and give one away
H elp in a way that cannot be repaid
A ct anonymously sometimes
R espect the receiver
I t will inspire others and multiply
T akes only a bit of selflessness
Y ou will feel a joy like no other

CANDLE
What we do today could be the **CANDLE** in someone else's darkness.

C alming voice
A cknowledging nod
N eeded smile
D etermined effort
L eading example
E ncouraging word

COUNT ON ME
When a friend is in need, one way to be a **COUNT ON ME** friend is to:

C ome without being asked
O pen the ears, not the mouth
U nconditionally support
N ever judgemental
T alk honestly when asked

O ffer advice gently
N avigate options with them

M aybe just be there
E ngage with encouragement

This is a lesson from my mother.

MEMORIAL*
I choose:

M emories of good times
E xcited to celebrate her life
M aintain focus on her gifts
O ptimistic above all
R emember what made her unique
I nspired to keep her memory alive
A cknowledge the sadness
L ift her up

Written for a dear friend who passed away recently.

KIND
If one person performed one **KIND** act to two people in one day and those two did the same, who did the same, who did the same and so on, in thirty days, over one billion lives would be touched with kindness.

K now your kindness matters
I mprove the day of someone today
N ow encourage them to do the same
D o it again—watch the world change

LIGHT (or two)
Today be someone's LIGHT and your life will light up too!

L ove	L ove
I nspire	I nspired
G ive	G raciousness
H ope	H appiness
T each!	T ogetherness

Today, let your LIGHT shine brightly and share it.

HUMAN
Be HUMAN about our journey.

H umbly proceed
U se the Golden Rule
M arch hard and step gently
A ccept uniqueness
N urture others

HEARTFELT
Let's make every day HEARTFELT and filled with:

H appiness
E nergy
A cts of kindness
R espect of self and others
T rust and trustworthiness
F riendship
E ncouragement to others
L ove, love, and love
T houghtfulness

SUPPORT
Today, let's SUPPORT each other.

S incerely
U plift
P eople
P ositively
O ffering
R espect
T houghtfulness

BLESSED
It is easy to help someone feel **BLESSED**. Let them know they are:

B eing
L oved
E very
S ingle
S econd
E very
D ay

CARE
When someone in our life needs us, here is one way to show we **CARE**.

C onnect on a personal level
A lign with the situation
R espect their perspective
E mpathize, don't try to fix

Sometimes it's just about being there.

CHILDREN
What is our responsibility as adults regarding **CHILDREN**?

C oaching
H elping
I nspiring
L oving
D eveloping
R especting
E ncouraging
N urturing

PRAISE
I believe we should **PRAISE** others, especially children and young adults, whenever we see good work. Here is one way to make remarks meaningful and memorable to the recipient.

P urposefully
R ecognize
A ctions
I ncluding
S pecific
E xamples

Words have a strong and lasting impact on others. Let's choose them carefully.

FRIEND
To have a friend, first be a **FRIEND**. Here are some ways to be one. Be:

F air
R espectful
I nspirational
E ncouraging
N urturing
D edicated

SPARK
Only takes a **SPARK** to light a fire. You never know when will have the opportunity to be the **SPARK** in someone's life. Look for that opportunity today!

S haring
P ositive
A ttitude
R einforcing
K indness

PHILANTHROPY
Today, do something nice for someone in a way they will never know you did it or can't repay you. I bet it will make you feel great inside! Could change a life! **PHILANTHROPY** is when you:

P ut someone else first
H elp those in need
I t isn't about me
L ove without condition
A ct out of kindness
N urture
T reat others with respect
H ave a passion for compassion
R each deeply and give from the heart
O pen doors for others
P ut yourself in their shoes
Y our rewards will surpass your sacrifice

ENCOURAGE
Look for opportunities to **ENCOURAGE** others.

E ngage
N urture
C oach
O ptimism
U plift
R eenforce
G uide
E nlighten

REFRESHING
Be **REFRESHING** to someone today.

R eady with a smile
E xtend a helping hand
F ree of judgement
R espectful of the situation
E mpathetic
S hare an encouraging word
H elpful in a meaningful way
I nterested in THEM
N urturing
G ive just to give

OTHERS
Think of **OTHERS** with your actions.

O utreach somehow
T ouch someone's need
H elp without asking how
E ncourage with a hug
R each beyond your bounds
S eek to make a new connection

INVOLVED
Get **INVOLVED** with something that improves your community. Each person's individual effort collectively makes a difference in the world.

I nvolve yourself with a helping cause
N o excuses, no giving up
V oice your opinions through constructive actions
O pen your heart and mind to selflessness
L ove without judgement
V isualize the difference you will make
E xpect setbacks, yet push onward
D edicate yourself to making a difference

IMPACT
Commit to making an **IMPACT**.

I mprove every situation we encounter
M otivate others by our actions
P rovide positive energy
A dvocate a "yes, we can" attitude
C hallenge ourselves to always improve
T reat others with respect and acceptance

GENEROUS
We all have an excess of something which others may need. Be **GENEROUS** with something today.

G ive
E xcessively
N ever
E xpecting
R eturn
O n
U nselfish
S haring

GENEROUS (times 2)
Thinking about the meaning of being **GENEROUS**, I've been the recipient of others' generosity and try to do the same when I have the opportunity.

G ifts are meant to be shared
E specially God-given ones
N ever for getting in return
E nriches the giver
R esets perspective of all
O thers come first
U sing our talents as a source
S miling might be the best gift of all

SUNSHINE
Be a little **SUNSHINE** for someone today.

S tand
U p (for someone in need)
N ow
S mile and
H elp
I nspire someone who
N eeds
E ncouragement

15

MANAGING EMOTIONS:
WHOA NELLIE...

How do we think first and act second? One way is to realize that often our emotions come to the surface first. They are often reactions from the heart and the gut. Sometimes they come out of survival instinct, a result of a perceived threat. Initial reactions in many cases are AWESOME and exactly the way to deal with situations. Other times they lead to a rush of judgement, an outburst, or action that in the long run, might not be what we intended nor what the situation called for. Installing the "wait a minute" or "Whoa Nellie" filter before jumping into action, can give the right amount of pause and enable us to call on the voice of reason in an emotional setting.

LOVE
LOVE. When we find it, we have to trust it, nurture it, and cherish it.

L ets down its protective guard
O pens itself to possibilities
V ulnerable like nothing else
E xposed to emotion's full vigor

Life's most powerful emotion: LOVE. What does LOVE mean to you?

MINDFUL
How we manage our MIND is crucial to our outlook, our attitude, our performance, and our outcomes.

Be **MINDFUL** of what we allow into the mind and out of our mouth.

M icromanage the inputs
I ngest only what will help
N ullify negative
D edicate the mind to possibilities
F ocus on the limitless
U se calming skills
L oosen the grip and enjoy

FEELINGS
FEELINGS are reactions we choose in a particular situation. Control them and we control our outlook.

F ace any situation with self-control
E valuate the significance quickly
E liminate the knee-jerk response
L isten with the heart and the mind
I nsist on always remaining hopeful
N ow choose how to respond
G et on with it, don't dwell
S et your feelings, control the outlook

FORGIVE
Sometimes FOR us to GIVE ourselves a fresh start, we have to FOR-GIVE ourselves for things in the past.

F ree ourselves from self-fault
O kay as we are
R ejoice in what we can become
G ive ourselves a serious break
I gnite ourselves in a new direction
V anish any limitations
E mbrace possibilities

DEPRESSION
Fight **DEPRESSION.**

D o
E verything
P ossible
R aising
E motions
S o
S trongly
I ntentionally
O bliterating
N egative

ANGER
We have all experienced **ANGER**. I have learned two lessons.

A
N o
G ood
E nergy
R obber

And **ANGER** is one letter away from **ANGEL**. And the world needs less **ANGER** and more **ANGEL's** work

STRESSED
When you start feeling **STRESSED**:

S tep away for a moment
T ake a look at the big picture
R emember God is with us
E mploy your strengths
S ettle your mind and emotion
S ee the outcome you seek
E mbark on what you CAN control
D ecide you will emerge successful

And remember **STRESSED** spelled backwards is DESSERTS! Use moderation.

DOUBT 1
You can be successful without a **DOUBT**.

D oes no good to the process
O ught to be eliminated
U seless to the cause
B etter silenced from the start
T erminated for good

Leave the **DOUBT OUT**!

DOUBT 2
Sometimes in stressful situations, **DOUBT** can emerge, causing us to question our ability to perform. Here is an idea if you feel **DOUBT**.

D ouble down on believing in yourself
O xygen is your friend. BREATHE!
U se your resources to fight negative
B elieve you will prevail then act
T alk positively to yourself always

16

LEADING ≠ MANAGING: DO WHAT LEADERS DO

There is plenty of research and writing about about leadership. Libraries are filled with theories and practices of the world's great leaders of state, business, the arts, sports, and academics. This chapter lists some of the qualities admirable of leaders. Leaders aren't always the boss, head coach, dean, CEO, senior partner, or anyone else with positions of control and power. Strive to be a leader everyday through your own actions and deeds. Develop and foster quality leadership skills. They will serve you and others well.

LEADERSHIP
On **LEADERSHIP.**

L ook for the opportunity
E ncourage others with your vision
A cknowledge leadership takes risk
D o it with humility
E ngage (roll up your sleeves)
R espect (earn it by doing)
S hare the rewards of success
H elp others help themselves
I nspire with compassion
P repare others to lead

AGILITY
I respect the **AGILITY** of dancers and other athletes. What about in life situations?

A daptable to change
G uided by strong values
I nquisitive of things to come
L ight and quick on the feet and mind
I nvolved in the moment yet with an eye on the future
T aking in the surroundings
Y ielding (under control and never on full throttle)

AGILE
Being AGILE.

Often we think of being AGILE only in dance or sports. An AGILE mind can lead to new opportunities and discover creative ways to solutions.

A nticipate and don't hesitate
G et relaxed in tense situations
I gnite possibility thinking
L et the mind and body align
E xpect the need to respond quickly

DECISIONS
Life continues to be driven by the DECISIONS we make. Make thoughtful DECISIONS because they impact everything.

D etermine our direction
E ngulf our thinking
C reate our opportunities
I nspire our actions
S et our attitude
I nfluence our expectations
O pen doors and leads to more decisions
N eed to be from the head and heart
S hould never be compromised

PACE
The happiness journey for me requires setting a good personal PACE, meaning:

P ersistent, patient, and positive
A ctionable, aware, and accepting
C onsistent, confident, and coachable
E ngaged, energized, and expectant

CHAMPION
Trophies don't define CHAMPIONS—actions do.

C omes and gives all they have everyday
H as respect for the game of life
A lways works on improving
M akes those around them better
P repares mentally and physically
I nsists on honesty and integrity
O pens up to coaching
N ever gives up

Outcome defines it for others. Effort defines it for ourselves.

STRETCHING
Ever thought about how **STRETCHING** provides flexibility to the body?
This applies to my mind as well.

S ome things start out painful
T oo difficult to grasp or do
R eally seem unattainable
E ventually with enough effort
T hings seem more within reach
C ausing the difficulty and pain to ease
H aving newfound confidence
I ncreases the possibilities
N ow we can see solutions
G rowth occurs and we have stretched ourselves

COACHABLE
My father encouraged me to stay **COACHABLE.**

C onfident yet humble
O pen to advice
A lways be listening
C heck the ego at the door
H ave respect for the teacher
A ccept the lesson
B e willing to change
L ife will teach us
E mpower yourself to let go to grow

MATTERS
Life improves each day when we find and do what **MATTERS.** What
MATTERS to you?

M akes a difference to others
A ttracts positive energy
T eaches something important
T ouches another's life positively
E levates the good
R echarges the spirit
S hares more than it gets

UTILITY
Often there is a feeling to be in complete control. There is often the need to just be a UTILITY player.

U se a skill to fill a specific role
T ackle the task as critical
I llustrate team play
L ook for ways to connect to others
I nsist on best effort
T ie into the big picture
Y our contribution matters

CHARACTER
What are the characteristics of CHARACTER?

C ares for others through actions.
H as no expectations of paybacks
A lways tries to do the right thing
R esponds before being asked
A pproaches problems with solutions, not blame
C harity comes to mind first
T akes on more of the load than required
E xpects nothing in return
R eaches with a hand out, not looking for a handout

BACKUP
Plan to be moving forward always, but always have a BACKUP plan.

B e ready to use it, but expect not to
A llow your actions to stay positive
C onfidently know you are prepared
K eep moving on with determination
U se your fortitude and intuition
P ut it in place, ONLY if necessary

A BACKUP plan reduces the risk of committing to the change we want for ourselves.

MEASURE
How to MEASURE progress?

M aking strides to a worthy goal
E ach day starts with positive vibes
A lways encouraging yourself
S taying focused on the target
U plifted even during a setback
R eaching further each day
E njoying the journey

GROWTH
The strongest trees are planted in the deepest holes. When we feel like we're in a hole, a rut, or a low place, reach for the sun and say, "It's time for GROWTH."

G reet the challenge with a smile
R each first for an obtainable goal, then set another
O bliterate your self-doubts
W ork on what really matters to you
T ell yourself the work is worth it—REPEAT
H ave the belief you will succeed

FIERCE
Be FIERCE in your purpose.

F ocused on the goal
I ncapable of distraction
E xpressly committed
R esouceful in new ways
C onfident in our abilities
E ncouraged regardless

EFFORT
Rarely have I done something well without putting in the hard work required to achieve the level of performance desired. I receive and appreciate that which comes with real EFFORT.

E mbrace the work required
F ind a way to self-motivate
F orget about taking shortcuts
O wn the input needed for the output desired
R efuse to settle until satisfied
T ackle the work with gusto and vigor

WINNER
What makes a WINNER?

W orks diligently to achieve worthy goals
I s focused and committed to reach them
N urtures the habit of focus
N o to negative
E xpects success from the onset
R efuses to give up, EVER

HONEST
When I was a child, I would get in more trouble for lying about what I did than for doing what I did. The lesson was be **HONEST**.

H ave the courage to be truthful
O perate with integrity
N o excuses, no surprises
E mbrace the honor of being truthful
S tick with the facts
T ake responsibility for our actions

HONESTY
Live with **HONESTY**.

H ave
O ne
N ever-changing
E xpectation
S imply be
T ruthful to
Y ourself and others

SUCCESS
In the world of sensationalized, media-hyped instant success, it's easy to forget that real **SUCCESS** comes from:

S ustained effort
U nrelenting commitment
C lear sense of purpose
C hallenges met head on
E xpectations of victory through work
S hared lessons learned on the way
S eeing the effort through the end

Let's teach this to our kids and grandkids.

SWEET
In life, we all have a **SWEET** spot where we do well, learn, and grow at the same time.

S ome place in your soul
W here you do your best work
E verything seems to click in place
E ffort produces great results
T oday seek to live from that place

ACCOMPLISHMENT
A single **ACCOMPLISHMENT** big or small means you can do ANY-THING you set your mind to!

A chieve anything you believe in
C onfidence is key
C oachability is essential
O ptimism trumps all emotions
M otivation grows with repetition
P ositive mindset is infectious
L ead yourself, set your example
I nsist on working harder when things are toughest
S eek small improvements
H ave more confidence daily
M ake yourself believe in you
E xpect the result you picture
N ever ever give up
T ell yourself, "Yes, I can."

ACCOMPLISHMENT today was the 365th message, making one message each day for a year. This process has inspired me to be a better person and hopefully inspire others.

PLANTING
If we keep **PLANTING** and tending to the seeds of goals and aspirations, we will always have a crop of opportunity. Never stop **PLANTING**.

P lant your goals in fertile soil
L abor in your garden of aspirations
A pply hard work until it hurts, repeat
N urture your dreams to the harvest
T ill the garden and plant again
I nvest in improving your soil
N ow replant with newer crops in mind
G oal reaching is the natural result

Today is another great day in life's garden.

PREPARE
While we can't be perfectly ready for every situation, we can **PREPARE**
to deal with the unexpected.

P ut ourselves in a good mindset
R ealize dealing with challenges IS life
E xpect the unexpected, don't dwell
P ractice being strong, repeat often
A ct with quiet confidence regardless
R ejoice in your faith and effort
E xcel because you are PREPARED

PREPARE a little each day.

PREPARE (some more)
Want luck? **PREPARE** for it!

P ut forth
R eal
E ffort
P ositive
A ffirmations with
R ealistic
E xpectations

Luck will take care of itself.

POSSIBLE
What's **POSSIBLE** if we commit ourselves to our goals and dreams?

P ossibilities become probabilities
O bstacles become opportunities
S truggles become stepping-stones
S ays who becomes says you
I mpossible becomes inevitable
B arely becomes bountiful
L aborious becomes a labor of love
E xcuses becomes excellence

NOURISH
In order to flourish when things get tough, we must **NOURISH** the right stuff.

N othing will be easy but will be worth it
O wn the outcome we want
U se every bit of energy we have
R each inside to stay the course
I nsist on getting where we want
S ettle for nothing less than the goal
H ave confidence in ourselves and faith in God

TEACH
A moment to **TEACH** our children can present itself at any time. Here is a way to seize and make the most of these moments.

T alk and listen, but listen more
E mpathize and encourage
A sk don't tell, let them self-teach
C hoose calmness as the tone
H elp more, holler less

Look for **TEACH**ing moments.

COURAGE
What does **COURAGE** mean to you? To me:

"C an do" in "no win" situations
O verlooks obstacles
U nstoppable determination
R eal action overtakes doubt
A ware of risks but does it any way
G ets over fear, goes on regardless
E xpects to be the exception to everyone's inevitable

We can all use a little more **COURAGE**.

MISTAKES
MISTAKES are the biggest teachers in life. We all make them. The best of us learn from them.

M ade to test and grow us
I nvaluable to the journey
S trengthen the survivors
T each, teach, and teach
A voidable only if no risk is taken
K eep us true to reality
E nable us to toughen up
S eparate players from spectators

Be a player in life. Make **MISTAKES**.

MISTAKES (more)
MISTAKES learned from can lead to riding an escalator vs. climbing a rope. Go ahead and take the risk of making some good ones to avoid future rope burns.

M ake the most of every opportunity
I nsist on letting go of fear
S tay confident and coachable
T ake advice with humility
A llow your thinking to stretch
K eep a sense of humor
E xpect some bumps and bruises
S ee the lesson beyond the error

INSPIRE
Today, oh to **INSPIRE**.

I mprove yourself
N urture others
S upport effort
P raise good
I nfuse positivity
R espect everyone
E ncourage progress

OPPORTUNITY
If we can open our minds and hearts to possibilities, opportunities emerge. Try opening up to **OPPORTUNITY** today.

O ptimistic
P ositive
P urpose
O pens
R eal
T angible
U nprecedented
N ew
I nsight
T o
Y ou

EXAMPLE
Lead by **EXAMPLE**.

E stablish the expectatins
eX amine my own actions
A lign my actions and expectations
M entor through life's experiences
P repare for the teaching process
L et go and grant responsibility
E xpect only the action I display

PLAN B
A good **PLAN B** is equally important to success as a good Plan A.

P rovides confidence to perform
L ets us totally GO FOR Plan A
A ssures a backup plan is there
N ot always used but always needed

B uilds a keen sense of preparation

LESSON (the LIFE kind)
Life **LESSON**: when the mouth is closed and the mind is opened, great things can happen!

L istening should trump talking
E ngage with questions vs. statements
S tay quiet and encourage
S eek to understand first
O ffer advice in moderation
N ow share the **LESSON**

BASICS
A simple but critical life skill is to do the **BASICS** well.

B elieve in yourself
A lways give 100 percent
S tay coachable
I nsist on being better each day
C hoose to be positive
S ee life as full of possibilities

TEAMWORK
TEAMWORK can get more accomplished.

T ogether
E veryone
A chieves
M ore
W hen
O ffering
R espect and
K indness

ABOUT THE AUTHOR

Bruce Pulver was inspired to create this book as words of inspiration for others and in order to help change lives. Bruce is passionate about self-improvement and is committed to learning and investing in helping others reach their goals and aspirations. Through his own growth and transformation, Bruce has seen his personal results reach increasingly greater levels. Bruce's personally developed habit of positive messaging has naturally bled over into the conversations with his family and created a mechanism to share his experience and lessons with others. As parents of two teenage daughters, Bruce and his wife Brigette keep busy with many school, sports, and arts activities.

MEET BRUCE PULVER

at

www.abovethechatterourwordsmatter.com

- Read his Blog

- Contact Bruce about speaking at your next event

- Connect to links for other personal growth resources

- "Like" Abovethechatterourwordsmatter on Facebook

- Follow Bruce @Abovethechatter on Twitter

- and more...

CPSIA information can be obtained at www.ICGtesting.com
Printed in the USA
LVOW06s0921120815

449801LV00003B/3/P